D0007173

ECLECTIC EDUCATIONAL SERIES.

M^CGUFFEY'S®

THIRD

ECLECTIC READER.

REVISED EDITION.

McGuffey Editions and Colophon are Trademarks of
VAN NOSTRAND REINHOLD COMPANY INC.
New York   Cincinnati   Toronto   London   Melbourne

PREFACE.

THE long-continued popularity of McGuffey's Readers is sufficient evidence of the positive merits of the books. The aim of this revision has been to preserve unimpaired the distinctive features of the series, and at the same time to present the matter in a new dress, with new type, new illustrations, and with a considerable amount of new matter.

Spelling exercises are continued through the first half of the THIRD READER. These exercises, with those furnished in the two lower books, are exhaustive of the words employed in the reading lessons. Words are not repeated in the vocabularies.

In the latter half of the book, definitions are introduced. It is hoped that the teacher will extend this defining exercise to all the words of the lesson liable to be misunderstood. The child should define the word in his own language sufficiently to show that he has a mastery of the word in its use.

Drills in articulation and emphasis should be given with every lesson. The essentials of good reading are not to be taught by one or two lessons. Constant drill on good exercises, with frequent exhibitions of the correct method from the teacher, will be found more effectual than any form prescribed in type.

If the pupils are not familiar with the diacritical marks, they should be carefully taught; such instruction constitutes an excellent drill on articulation, and enables the pupils to use the dictionary with intelligence.

Copyright, 1879, by VAN ANTWERP, BRAGG & CO.
Copyright, 1896, by AMERICAN BOOK COMPANY.
Copyright, 1907 and 1920, by H. H. VAIL.

M'G. 3D 50 REV.

EP 300

CONTENTS

INTRODUCTION.

ARTICULATION.

A distinct articulation can only be gained by constant and careful practice of the elementary sounds.

Whenever a word is imperfectly enunciated, the teacher should call attention to the *sounds* composing the spoken word.

If the pupil fails to sound any element correctly, as in the case of lisping, the fault can be overcome by calling attention to the correct position of the organs of speech, and insisting upon exact execution. Except in case of malformation of these organs, every pupil should sound each element correctly before such drill should cease.

TABLE OF VOCALS.

LONG SOUNDS.

ā,	as in	āte.		ẽ,	as in	ẽrr.
â,	"	eâre.		ī,	"	īçe.
ä,	"	ärm.		ŏ,	"	ŏde.
ȧ,	"	lȧst.		ū,	"	tūne.
a̤,	"	a̤ll.		û,	"	bûrn.
ē,	"	ēve.		o͞o,	"	fo͞ol.

SHORT SOUNDS.

ă, as in ăm.   ŏ, as in ŏdd.
ĕ, "   ĕlm.   ŭ, "   ŭp.
ĭ, "   ĭn.   ŏŏ, "   lŏŏk.

DIPHTHONGS.

oi, as in oil. | ou, as in out.

TABLE OF SUBVOCALS.

b, as in bĭb.   v, as in vălve.
d, "   dĭd.   th, "   thĭs.
g, "   ḡĭḡ.   z, "   zīne.
j, "   jŭḡ.   z, "   ăzure.
n, "   nīne.   r, "   râre.
m, "   māim.   w, "   wē.
ng, "   hăng.   y, "   yĕt.

l, as in lŭll.

TABLE OF ASPIRATES.

f, as in fīfe.   t, as in tärt.
h, "   hĭm.   sh, "   shē.
k, "   eāke.   ch, "   chăt.
p, "   pīpe.   th, "   thĭck.
s, "   sāme.   wh, "   whȳ.

NOTE.—The above forty-five sounds are those most employed in the English language. Some of these sounds are represented by other letters, as shown in the following table.

TABLE OF SUBSTITUTES.

ạ, for ŏ, as in whạt.	y̆, for ĭ, as in my̆th.
ê, " â, " thêre.	e, " k, " eăn.
ẹ, " ā, " fẹint.	ç, " s, " çīte.
ï, " ē, " polïçe.	çh, " sh, " çhāiṣe.
ī, " ẽ, " sīr.	eh, " ᴋ, " ehāos.
ȯ, " ŭ, " sȯn.	ġ, " j, " ġĕm.
ọ, " ōō, " tọ.	ṉ, " ng, " ĭṉk.
o̦, " ŏ͞o, " wo̦lf.	ṣ, " z, " ăṣ.
ô, " ạ, " fôrk.	s, " sh, " sṳre.
õ, " û, " wõrk.	x̱, " g̅z, " ĕx̱ăet.
ṳ, " ŏ͞o, " fṳll.	gh, " f, " läugh.
u̱, " ōō, " ru̱de.	ph, " f, " phlŏx.
ȳ, " ī, " flȳ.	qu, " k, " pïque.

qu, for kw, as in quĭt.

EXERCISES IN ARTICULATION.

The following exercises may be used for drill after the tables are fully understood. Pronounce the word first; then, the sound indicated.

EXERCISE I.

ā—āte,	fāte.	ē—mē,	shē.
ă—ăt,	hăt.	ĕ—mĕt,	wĕll.
â—çâre,	snâre.	ē—hēr,	jērk.
ä—ärm,	bärn.	ī—īçe,	kīte.
à—àsk,	pàst.	ĭ—ĭn,	bĭt.
ạ—ạll,	quạrt.	ī—sīr,	fīrm.

EXERCISE II.

ō—gō,	ōde.	ô—nôr,	môrn.
ŏ—hŏt,	plŏt.	ū—ūse,	tūne.
ọ—dọ,	mọve.	ŭ—ŭs,	tŭb.
ȯ—sȯn,	dȯne.	ų—pųt,	pųll.
ọ—wọlf,	wọman.	û—bûrn,	ûrġe.

EXERCISE III.

ōō—fōōl,	mōōn.	b—bābe,	Bīble.
ŏŏ—ḡŏŏd,	fŏŏt.	d—dĭd,	dăndy.
oi—oil,	boil.	f—ĭf,	fīfe.
oy—toy,	joy.	ḡ—ḡăḡ,	ḡīḡ.
ou—out,	loud.	h—hĭt,	hȯw.
ow—now,	owl.	j—jāy,	lärġe.

EXERCISE IV.

k —kīte,	eăn.	s —sau̯çe.	rīçe.
l —lăd,	pĭll.	t —tăt,	tōtal.
m —mä'am,	mŭm.	v —văn,	lŏve.
n —ĭn,	nīne.	w —wĭn,	wīde.
p —ăpple,	pīpe.	y —yĕs,	yo̯u.
r —râre,	rōar.	z —sīze,	wīṣe.

EXERCISE V.

Bl —blāde,	blĕd.	Dw—dwĕll,	dwạrf.
Br —brăd,	brīde.	Fl —flăt,	flee.
Bs —rŏbṣ,	fĭbṣ.	Fr —frāme,	frȳ.
Ch —chăt,	rĭch.	Fs —mŭffs,	läughs.
Dl —lādle,	săddle.	Gl —ḡlăd,	ḡlīde.
Dr —drăb,	drōne.	Gr —ḡreāt,	ḡrōw.
Ds —rĭdṣ,	bŭdṣ.	Kn —knee,	knōw.

EXERCISE VI.

Pl —plāte,	plŏt.	Sq —squạt,	squīrm.
Pr —prāy,	prōne.	St —stănd,	stōne.
Sh —shăll,	çhāiṣe.	Sw —swạrm,	swĭm.
Sl —slăp,	slōw.	Th —thĭck,	thĭn.
Sm—smärt,	smīte.	Th —thīne,	wĭth.
Sn —snâre,	snōw.	Tw. —twīçe,	twĕnty
Sp —spĭn,	spoil.	Wh—whĕn,	whĭch

EMPHASIS.

Note.--If the pupil has received proper oral instruction, he has been taught to *understand* what he has read, and has already acquired the *habit* of emphasizing words. He is now prepared for a more formal introduction to the subject of emphasis, and for more particular attention to its first principles. This lesson, and the examples given, should be repeatedly practiced.

In reading and in talking, we always speak some words with more force than others. We do this, because the meaning of what we say depends most upon these words.

If I wish to know whether it is George or his brother who is sick, I speak the words *George* and *brother* with more force than the other words. I say, Is it *George* or his *brother* who is sick?

This greater force with which we speak the words is called EMPHASIS.

The words upon which emphasis is put, are sometimes printed in slanting letters, called *Italics*,* and sometimes in CAPITALS.

The words printed in Italics in the following questions and answers, should be read with more force than the other words, that is, with emphasis.

Did *you* ride to town yesterday? No, my *brother* did.

Did you *ride* to town yesterday? No, I *walked.*

Italics are also used for other purposes, though most frequently for emphasis.

Did you ride to *town* yesterday? No, I went into the *country*.

Did you ride to town *yesterday?* No, I went *the day before.*

Have you seen *James* or *John* lately? I have seen *James,* but not *John.*

Did you say there were *four* eggs in the nest, or *three?* There were only *three* eggs, not *four.*

Were the eggs *white* or *blue?* The eggs were *white,* not *blue.*

Had the boy a *hat* on his head, or a *cap?* He had a *cap* on, not a *hat.*

PUNCTUATION.

☞ PUNCTUATION should be thoroughly studied by the pupil, in order that he may become perfectly familiar with the marks and pauses found in the reading lessons of this volume.

MARKS AND PAUSES.

These marks are used to point off written or printed matter into sentences and parts of sentences, and thus to assist the reader in obtaining the meaning of the writer. They seldom indicate the length of the pause to be made; this must be determined by the sense.

A **Hyphen** (-) is used between syllables in a word divided at the end of a line; as, " be-cause," "ques-tion," page 10, and between the parts of a compound word; as,

Rocking-chair, good-by.

The **Comma** (,), **Semicolon** (;), and **Colon** (:) mark grammatical divisions in a sentence; as,

> God is good; for he gives us all things.
> Be wise to-day, my child: 't is madness to defer.

A **Period** (.) is placed at the end of a sentence; as,

> God is love.   Life is short.

Or is used after an abbreviation; as,

> Dr. Murphy.   Jan. 10, 1879.

An **Interrogation Point** (?) denotes a question; as,

> Has he come?   Who are you?

An **Exclamation Point** (!) denotes strong feeling; as,

> O Absalom! my son! my son!

The **Dash** (—) is used where there is a sudden break or pause in a sentence; as,

> The truth has power--such is God's will—to make us better.

Quotation Marks (" ") denote the words of another; as,

> God said, "Let there be light."

An **Apostrophe** (') denotes that a letter or letters are left out; as,

> O'er, for over; 't is, for it is.

And is also used to show ownership; as,

> The man's hat.   Helen's book.

McGUFFEY'S
THIRD READER.

LESSON I.

| ēi'ther | trĭe'kle | făn'çied | mûr'mur | re flĕet'ed |
| ḡlŏss'y | ĕn'tered | shĕp'herd | chĕst'nuts | eom mȧnd' |

THE SHEPHERD BOY.

1. Little Roy led his sheep down to pasture,
   And his cows, by the side of the brook;

(13)

But his cows never drank any water,
 And his sheep never needed a crook.

2. For the pasture was gay as a garden,
 And it glowed with a flowery red;
But the meadows had never a grass blade,
 And the brooklet — it slept in its bed:

3. And it lay without sparkle or murmur,
 Nor reflected the blue of the skies;
But the music was made by the shepherd,
 And the sparkle was all in his eyes.

4. Oh, he sang like a bird in the summer!
 And, if sometimes you fancied a bleat,
That, too, was the voice of the shepherd,
 And not of the lambs at his feet.

5. And the glossy brown cows were so gentle
 That they moved at the touch of his hand
O'er the wonderful, rosy-red meadow,
 And they stood at the word of command.

6. So he led all his sheep to the pasture,
 And his cows, by the side of the brook;
Though it rained, yet the rain never pattered
 O'er the beautiful way that they took.

7. And it was n't in Fairyland either,
 But a house in the midst of the town,
Where Roy, as he looked from the window,
 Saw the silvery drops trickle down.

8. For his pasture was only a table,
    With its cover so flowery fair,
  And his brooklet was just a green ribbon,
    That his sister had lost from her hair.

9. And his cows were but glossy horse-chestnuts,
    That had grown on his grandfather's tree;
  And his sheep only snowy-white pebbles,
    He had brought from the shore of the sea.

10. And at length when the shepherd was weary,
    And had taken his milk and his bread,
  And his mother had kissed him and tucked him,
    And had bid him "good night" in his bed;

11. Then there entered his big brother Walter,
    While the shepherd was soundly asleep,
  And he cut up the cows into baskets,
    And to jackstones turned all of the sheep.

Emily S. Oakey.

LESSON II.

eoŭn'try   ḡrōveṣ   loṣ'ing   sụḡ'ar   freez'eṣ

JOHNNY'S FIRST SNOWSTORM.

1. Johnny Reed was a little boy who never had seen a snowstorm till he was six years old. Before this, he had lived in a warm country, where the sun shines down on beautiful

orange groves, and fields always sweet with flowers.

2. But now he had come to visit his grandmother, who lived where the snow falls in winter. Johnny was standing at the window when the snow came down.

3. "O mamma!" he cried, joyfully, "do come quick, and see these little white birds flying down from heaven."

4. "They are not birds, Johnny," said mamma, smiling.

5. "Then maybe the little angels are losing their feathers! Oh! do tell me what it is; is it sugar? Let me taste it," said

Johnny. But when he tasted it, he gave a little jump—it was so cold.

6. "That is only snow, Johnny," said his mother.

7. "What is snow, mother?"

8. "The snowflakes, Johnny, are little drops of water that fall from the clouds. But the air through which they pass is so cold it freezes them, and they come down turned into snow."

9. As she said this, she brought out an old black hat from the closet. "See, Johnny! I have caught a snowflake on this hat. Look quick through this glass, and you will see how beautiful it is."

10. Johnny looked through the glass. There lay the pure, feathery snowflake like a lovely little star.

11. "Twinkle, twinkle, little star!" he cried in delight. "Oh! please show me more snow-flakes, mother."

12. So his mother caught several more, and they were all beautiful.

13. The next day Johnny had a fine play in the snow, and when he came in, he said, "I love snow; and I think snowballs are a great deal prettier than oranges."

3, 4

LESSON III.

dạugh'ter   quĕnch   wrēathş   bŭt'ter   thīrst'y

LET IT RAIN.

Rose. See how it rains! Oh dear, dear, dear! how dull it is! Must I stay in doors all day?

Father. Why, Rose, are you sorry that you had any bread and butter for breakfast, this morning?

Rose. Why, father, what a question! I should be sorry, indeed, if I could not get any.

Father. Are you sorry, my daughter, when you see the flowers and the trees growing in the garden?

Rose. Sorry? No, indeed. Just now, I wished very much to go out and see them, —they look so pretty.

Father. Well, are you sorry when you see the horses, cows, or sheep drinking at the brook to quench their thirst?

Rose. Why, father, you must think I am a cruel girl, to wish that the poor horses that work so hard, the beautiful cows that give so much nice milk, and the pretty lambs should always be thirsty.

Father. Do you not think they would die, if they had no water to drink?

Rose. Yes, sir, I am sure they would. How shocking to think of such a thing!

Father. I thought little Rose was sorry it rained. Do you think the trees and flowers would grow, if they never had any water on them?

Rose. No, indeed, father, they would be dried up by the sun. Then we should not have any pretty flowers to look at, and to make wreaths of for mother.

Father. I thought you were sorry it rained. Rose, what is our bread made of?

Rose. It is made of flour, and the flour is made from wheat, which is ground in the mill.

Father. Yes, Rose, and it was rain that helped to make the wheat grow, and it was water that turned the mill to grind the wheat. I thought little Rose was sorry it rained.

Rose. I did not think of all these things, father. I am truly very glad to see the rain falling.

LESSON IV.

ăṉ'ġer	eăs'tle	foun dā'tion	răt'tling	tow'er
dis māy'	sō'fà	ĭn'ter ĕst ed	păs'sion	pīle
mĭm'ie	nŏd'ded	ex elāimed'	ạl rĕad'y	spĭlled

CASTLE-BUILDING.

1. "O pussy!" cried Herbert, in a voice of anger and dismay, as the blockhouse he was building fell in sudden ruin. The play-ful cat had rubbed against his mimic castle,

and tower and wall went rattling down upon the floor.

2. Herbert took up one of the blocks and threw it fiercely at pussy. Happily, it passed over her and did no harm. His hand was reaching for another block, when his little sister Hetty sprang toward the cat, and caught her up.

3. "No, no, no!" said she, "you sha'n't hurt pussy! She did n't mean to do it!"

4. Herbert's passion was over quickly, and, sitting down upon the floor, he covered his face with his hands, and began to cry.

5. "What a baby!" said Joe, his elder brother, who was reading on the sofa. "Crying over spilled milk does no good. Build it up again."

6. "No, I won't," said Herbert, and he went on crying.

7. "What's all the trouble here?" exclaimed papa, as he opened the door and came in.

8. "Pussy just rubbed against Herbert's castle, and it fell down," answered Hetty. "But she did n't mean to do it; she did n't know it would fall, did she, papa?"

9. "Why, no! And is that all the trouble?"

10. "Herbert!" his papa called, and held out his hands. "Come." The little boy got up from the floor, and came slowly, his eyes full of tears, and stood by his father.

11. "There is a better way than this, my boy," said papa. "If you had taken that way, your heart would have been light already. I should have heard you singing over your blocks instead of crying. Shall I show you that way?"

12. Herbert nodded his head, and papa sat down on the floor by the pile of blocks, with his little son by his side, and began to lay the foundation for a new castle.

LESSON V.

| strĭng | pā′per | ēa′ḡer ly | dăshed | eāse |
| erăsh | dĭsh′eṣ | re tôrt′ed | sĕn′tençe | trāy |

CASTLE-BUILDING.

(CONCLUDED.)

1. Soon, Herbert was as much interested in castle-building as he had been a little while before. He began to sing over his work. All his trouble was gone.

2. "This is a great deal better than crying, is n't it?" said papa.

3. "Crying for what?" asked Herbert, forgetting his grief of a few minutes before.

4. "Because pussy knocked your castle over."

5. "Oh!" A shadow flitted across his face, but was gone in a moment, and he went on building as eagerly as ever.

6. "I told him not to cry over spilled milk," said Joe, looking down from his place on the sofa.

7. "I wonder if you did n't cry when your kite string broke," retorted Herbert.

8. "Losing a kite is quite another thing," answered Joe, a little dashed. "The kite was gone forever; but your blocks were as good as before, and you had only to build again."

9. "I do n't see," said papa, "that crying was of any more use in your case than in Herbert's. Sticks and paper are easily found, and you had only to go to work and make another kite." Joe looked down at his book, and went on reading. By this time the castle was finished.

10. "It is ever so much nicer than the one

pussy knocked down," said Hetty. And so thought Herbert, as he looked at it proudly from all sides.

11. "If pussy knocks that down, I'll—"

12. "Build it up again," said papa, finishing the sentence for his little boy.

13. "But, papa, pussy must not knock my castles down. I can't have it," spoke out Herbert, knitting his forehead.

14. "You must watch her, then. Little boys, as well as grown up people, have to be often on their guard. If you go into the street, you have to look out for the carriages, so as not to be run over, and you have to keep out of people's way.

15. "In the house, if you go about heed-lessly, you will be very apt to run against some one. I have seen a careless child dash suddenly into a room just as a servant was leaving it with a tray of dishes in her hands. A crash followed."

16. "It was I, wasn't it?" said Hetty.

17. "Yes, I believe it was, and I hope it will never happen again."

18. Papa now left the room, saying, "I don't want any more of this crying over spilled milk, as Joe says. If your castles get knocked down, build them up again."

LESSON VI.

teâr	dāi′ly	hŏn′or	tòngueṣ	sus pī′cion
ĕn′vy	fōrçed	prŏmpt	ma lĭ′cioŭs	to-mŏr′row

LEND A HAND.

I.

Lend a hand to one another
In the daily toil of life;
When we meet a weaker brother,
Let us help him in the strife.
There is none so rich but may,
In his turn, be forced to borrow;
And the poor man's lot to-day
May become our own to-morrow.

2.

Lend a hand to one another:
When malicious tongues have thrown
Dark suspicion on your brother,
Be not prompt to cast a stone.
There is none so good but may
Run adrift in shame and sorrow.
And the good man of to-day
May become the bad to-morrow.

3.

Lend a hand to one another:
In the race for Honor's crown;
Should it fall upon your brother.
Let not envy tear it down.
Lend a hand to all, we pray,
In their sunshine or their sorrow;
And the prize they've won to-day
May become our own to-morrow

LESSON VII.

fạlse'ly	at tĕnd'	trụ'ant	eŏn'duet	thêre'fōre
ḡuĭlt'y	hāste	rĕḡ'u lar	strŭḡ'ḡled	ĭḡ'no rant

THE TRUANT.

1. James Brown was ten years old when his parents sent him to school. It was not far from his home, and therefore they sent him by himself.

2. But, instead of going to school, he was in the habit of playing truant. He would go into the fields, or spend his time with idle boys.

3. But this was not all. When he went home, he would falsely tell his mother that he had been to school, and had said his lessons very well.

4. One fine morning, his mother told James to make haste home from school, for she wished, after he had come back, to take him to his aunt's.

5. But, instead of minding her, he went off to the water, where there were some boats. There he met plenty of idle boys.

6. Some of these boys found that James

had money, which his aunt had given him; and he was led by them to hire a boat, and to go with them upon the water.

7. Little did James think of the danger into which he was running. Soon the wind began to blow, and none of them knew how to manage the boat.

8. For some time, they struggled against the wind and the tide. At last, they became so tired that they could row no longer.

9. A large wave upset the boat, and they were all thrown into the water. Think of James Brown, the truant, at this time!

10. He was far from home, known by no one. His parents were ignorant of his danger.

He was struggling in the water, on the point of being drowned.

11. Some men, however, saw the boys, and went out to them in a boat. They reached them just in time to save them from a watery grave.

12. They were taken into a house, where their clothes were dried. After a while, they were sent home to their parents.

13. James was very sorry for his conduct, and he was never known to be guilty of the same thing again.

14. He became regular at school, learned to attend to his books, and, above all, to obey his parents perfectly.

LESSON VIII.

strōke   bĕḡ′ḡar   strēaks   need′fṳl   eoun′sel

THE WHITE KITTEN.

1. My little white kitten 's asleep on my knee;
   As white as the snow or the lilies is she;
       She wakes up with a pur
       When I stroke her soft fur:
   Was there ever another white kitten like her?

2. My little white kitten now wants to go out
   And frolic, with no one to watch her about;
   　　" Little kitten," I say,
   　　" Just an hour you may stay,
   And be careful in choosing your places to play."

3. But night has come down, when I hear a loud " mew; "
   I open the door, and my kitten comes through;
   　　My white kitten! ah me!
   　　Can it really be she—
   This ill-looking, beggar-like cat that I see?

4. What ugly, gray streaks on her side and her back!
   Her nose, once as pink as a rosebud, is black!
   　　Oh, I very well know,
   　　Though she does not say so,
   She has been where white kittens ought never to go.

5. If little good children intend to do right,
  If little white kittens would keep themselves white,
    It is needful that they
    Should this counsel obey,
  And be careful in choosing their places to play.

LESSON IX.

pre fĕr′	trăp′per	fôr′ward	ma tē′ri al	dis tûrb′ing
dŭmb	chiēf′ly	gnạw′ing	A mĕr′ĭ eȧ	eạu′tioŭs ly
heīght	pûr′pȯse	tīght′er	re mīnd′ed	frē′quent ly
ob tāin′	eū′ri oŭs	in hū′man	in elūd′ing	eon strŭet′ed

THE BEAVER.

1. The beaver is found chiefly in North America. It is about three and a half feet long, including the flat, paddle-shaped tail, which is a foot in length.

2. The long, shining hair on the back is chestnut-colored, while the fine, soft fur that lies next the skin, is grayish brown.

3. Beavers build themselves most curious huts to live in, and quite frequently a great number of these huts are placed close together, like the buildings in a town.

4. They always build their huts on the banks of rivers or lakes, for they swim much

more easily than they walk, and prefer moving about in the water.

5. When they build on the bank of a running stream, they make a dam across the stream for the purpose of keeping the water at the height they wish.

6. These dams are made chiefly of mud, and stones, and the branches of trees. They are sometimes six or seven hundred feet in length, and are so constructed that they look more like the work of man than of little dumb beasts.

7. Their huts are made of the same material as the dams, and are round in shape. The walls are very thick, and the roofs are finished off with a thick layer of mud, sticks, and leaves.

8. They commence building their houses late in the summer, but do not get them finished before the early frosts. The freezing makes them tighter and stronger.

9. They obtain the wood for their dams and huts by gnawing through the branches of trees, and even through the trunks of small ones, with their sharp front teeth. They peel off the bark, and lay it up in store for winter food.

10. The fur of the beaver is highly prized. The men who hunt these animals are called trappers.

11. A gentleman once saw five young beavers playing. They would leap on the trunk of a tree that lay near a beaver dam, and would push one another off into the water.

12. He crept forward very cautiously, and was about to fire on the little creatures; but their amusing tricks reminded him so much of some little children he knew at home, that he thought it would be inhuman to kill them. So he left them without even disturbing their play.

_{a, a.}

LESSON X.

sīgn	märks	pär'çelṣ	vĕn'ture	in quīre'
chȧlk	rṳl'ing	drạw'ing	pĭe'tureṣ	eon fūṣed'

THE YOUNG TEACHER.

1. Charles Rose lived in the country with his father, who taught him to read and to write.

2. Mr. Rose told his son that, when his morning lessons were over, he might amuse himself for one hour as he pleased.

3. There was a river near by. On its bank stood the hut of a poor fisherman, who lived by selling fish.

4. His careful wife kept her wheel going early and late. They both worked very hard to keep themselves above want.

5. But they were greatly troubled lest their only son should never learn to read and to write. They could not teach him themselves, and they were too poor to send him to school.

6. Charles called at the hut of this fisherman one day, to inquire about his dog, which was missing.

7. He found the little boy, whose name was Joe, sitting by the table, on which he was making marks with a piece of chalk.

Charles asked him whether he was drawing pictures.

8. "No, I am trying to write," said little Joe, "but I know only two words. Those I saw upon a sign, and I am trying to write them."

9. "If I could only learn to read and write," said he, "I should be the happiest boy in the world."

10. "Then I will make you happy," said Charles. "I am only a little boy, but I can teach you that.

11. "My father gives me an hour every day for myself. Now, if you will try to learn, you shall soon know how to read and to write."

12. Both Joe and his mother were ready to fall on their knees to thank Charles. They told him it was what they wished above all things.

13. So, on the next day when the hour came, Charles put his book in his pocket, and went to teach Joe. Joe learned very fast, and Charles soon began to teach him how to write.

14. Some time after, a gentleman called on Mr. Rose, and asked him if he knew where Charles was. Mr. Rose said that he was taking a walk, he supposed.

15. "I am afraid," said the gentleman, "that he does not always amuse himself thus. I often see him go to the house of the fisherman. I fear he goes out in their boat."

16. Mr. Rose was much troubled. He had told Charles that he must never venture

on the river, and he thought he could trust him.

17. The moment the gentleman left, Mr. Rose went in search of his son. He went to the river, and walked up and down, in hope of seeing the boat.

18. Not seeing it, he grew uneasy. He thought Charles must have gone a long way off. Unwilling to leave without learning something of him, he went to the hut.

19. He put his head in at the window, which was open. There a pleasant sight met his eyes.

20. Charles was at the table, ruling a copybook. Joe was reading to him, while his mother was spinning in the corner.

21. Charles was a little confused. He feared his father might not be pleased; but he had no need to be uneasy, for his father was delighted.

22. The next day, his father took him to town, and gave him books for himself and Joe, with writing paper, pens, and ink.

23. Charles was the happiest boy in the world when he came home. He ran to Joe, his hands filled with parcels, and his heart beating with joy.

LESSON XI.

ī′ron (ī′urn)
eȳe′ lĭds̱
fōrġe
in tĕnse′

elĭn̲′ker ty
shrĭn̲k
lă′bor
hăm′mer

THE BLACKSMITH.

1. Clink, clink, clinkerty clink!
  We begin to hammer at morning's blink,
      And hammer away
      Till the busy day,
  Like us, aweary, to rest shall sink.

2. Clink, clink, clinkerty clink!
  From labor and care we never will shrink;
      But our fires we'll blow
      Till our forges glow
  With light intense, while our eyelids wink.

3. Clink, clink, clinkerty clink?
   The chain we'll forge with many a link.
      We'll work each form
      While the iron is warm,
   With strokes as fast as we can think.

4. Clink, clink, clinkerty clink!
   Our faces may be as black as ink,
      But our hearts are true
      As man ever knew,
   And kindly of all we shall ever think.

LESSON XII.

shŏŏk	grāv′el	in vīt′ed	as sure′	eon tĭn′ūed
plănts	bôr′ders	en joyed′	mĕd′dle	ad mīr′ing

A WALK IN THE GARDEN.

1. Frank was one day walking with his mother, when they came to a pretty garden. Frank looked in, and saw that it had clean gravel walks, and beds of beautiful flowers all in bloom.

2. He called to his mother, and said, "Mother, come and look at this pretty garden. I wish I might open the gate, and walk in."

3. The gardener, being near, heard what Frank said, and kindly invited him and his mother to come into the garden.

4. Frank's mother thanked the man. Turning to her son, she said, "Frank, if I take you to walk in this garden, you must take care not to meddle with anything in it."

5. Frank walked along the neat gravel paths, and looked at everything, but touched nothing that he saw.

6. He did not tread on any of the borders, and was careful that his clothes should not brush the tops of the flowers, lest he might break them.

7. The gardener was much pleased with Frank, because he was so careful not to do mischief. He showed him the seeds, and told him the names of many of the flowers and plants.

8. While Frank was admiring the beauty of a flower, a boy came to the gate, and finding it locked, he shook it hard. But it would not open. Then he said, " Let me in; let me in; will you not let me in this garden ? "

9. "No, indeed," said the gardener, "I will not let you in, I assure you; for when I let you in yesterday, you meddled with my flowers, and pulled some of my rare fruit. I do not choose to let a boy into my garden who meddles with the plants."

10. The boy looked ashamed, and when he found that the gardener would not let him in, he went slowly away.

11. Frank saw and felt how much happier a boy may be by not meddling with what does not belong to him.

12. He and his mother then continued their walk in the garden, and enjoyed the day very much. Before they left, the gardener gave each of them some pretty flowers.

LESSON XIII.

woļf	ḡriēved	sleeve	nẹigh′borş	ẽar′nest
ăx′eş	elŭbş	ôr′der	sĭn′ḡle	de stroy′

THE WOLF.

1. A boy was once taking care of some sheep, not far from a forest. Near by was a village, and he was told to call for help if there was any danger.

2. One day, in order to have some fun, he cried out, with all his might, "The wolf is coming! the wolf is coming!"

3. The men came running with clubs and axes to destroy the wolf. As they saw nothing they went home again, and left John laughing in his sleeve.

4. As he had had so much fun this time, John cried out again, the next day, "The wolf! the wolf!"

5. The men came again, but not so many as the first time. Again they saw no trace of the wolf; so they shook their heads, and went back.

6. On the third day, the wolf came in earnest. John cried in dismay, "Help! help!

the wolf! the wolf!" But not a single man came to help him.

7. The wolf broke into the flock, and killed

a great many sheep. Among them was a beautiful lamb, which belonged to John.

8. Then he felt very sorry that he had deceived his friends and neighbors, and grieved over the loss of his pet lamb.

> The truth itself is not believed,
> From one who often has deceived.

LESSON XIV.

měl'o dy　　un nō'tǐçed　　mǒd'est　　eon těnt'　　Grā'çie

THE LITTLE BIRD'S SONG.

1. A little bird, with feathers brown,
   Sat singing on a tree;
   The song was very soft and low,
   But sweet as it could be.

2. The people who were passing by,
   Looked up to see the bird

That made the sweetest melody
    That ever they had heard.

3. But all the bright eyes looked in vain;
    Birdie was very small,
And with his modest, dark-brown coat,
    He made no show at all.

4. "Why, father," little Gracie said,
    "Where can the birdie be?
If I could sing a song like that,
    I'd sit where folks could see."

5. "I hope my little girl will learn
    A lesson from the bird,
And try to do what good she can,
    Not to be seen or heard.

6. "This birdie is content to sit
    Unnoticed on the way,
And sweetly sing his Maker's praise
    From dawn to close of day.

7. "So live, my child, all through your life,
    That, be it short or long,
Though others may forget your looks,
    They'll not forget your song."

LESSON XV.

lēast	thạw	slīd′ing	plŭnġed	nāt′ured ly
bă̆de	seă̆t′ter	pre tĕnd′	ex plōr′ing	dĭs o bē′di ent

HARRY AND ANNIE.

1. Harry and Annie lived a mile from town, but they went there to school every day. It was a pleasant walk down the lane, and through the meadow by the pond.

2. I hardly know whether they liked it better in summer or in winter. They used to pretend that they were travelers exploring a new country, and would scatter leaves on

the road that they might find their way back again.

3. When the ice was thick and firm, they went across the pond. But their mother did not like to have them do this unless some one was with them.

4. "Don't go across the pond to-day, children," she said, as she kissed them and bade them good-by one morning; "it is beginning to thaw."

5. "All right, mother," said Harry, not very good-naturedly, for he was very fond of running and sliding on the ice. When they came to the pond, the ice looked hard and safe.

6. "There," said he to his sister, "I knew it hadn't thawed any. Mother is always afraid we shall be drowned. Come along, we will have a good time sliding. The school bell will not ring for an hour at least."

7. "But you promised mother," said Annie.

8. "No, I didn't. I only said 'All right,' and it *is* all right."

9. "I didn't say anything; so I can do as I like," said Annie.

10. So they stepped on the ice, and started to go across the pond. They had not gone

far before the ice gave way, and they fell into the water.

11. A man who was at work near the shore, heard the screams of the children, and plunged into the water to save them. Harry managed to get to the shore without any help, but poor Annie was nearly drowned before the man could reach her.

12. Harry went home almost frozen, and told his mother how disobedient he had been. He remembered the lesson learned that day as long as he lived.

LESSON XVI.

wīfe	ḡreet	bĕard	wõrmṣ	prâyerṣ
fāith	ḡrōve	erŭsts	chûrch	fûr′nished

BIRD FRIENDS.

1. I once knew a man who was rich in his love for birds, and in their love for him. He lived in the midst of a grove full of all kinds of trees. He had no wife or children in his home.

2. He was an old man with gray beard, blue and kind eyes, and a voice that the

birds loved; and this was the way he made
them his friends.

3. While he was at work with a rake on
his nice walks in the grove, the birds came

close to him to pick up the worms in the
fresh earth he dug up. At first, they kept
a rod or two from him, but they soon found
he was a kind man, and would not hurt
them, but liked to have them near him.

4. They knew this by his kind eyes **and** voice, which tell what is in the heart. So, day by day their faith in his love grew in them.

5. They came close to the rake. They would hop on top of it, to be first at the worm. They would turn up their eyes into his when he spoke to them, as if they said, "He is a kind man; he loves us; we need not fear him."

6. All the birds of the grove were soon his fast friends. They were on the watch for him, and would fly down from the green tree tops to greet him with their chirp.

7. When he had no work on the walks to do with his rake or his hoe, he took crusts of bread with him, and dropped the crumbs on the ground. Down they would dart on his head and feet to catch them as they fell from his hand.

8 He showed me how they loved him. He put a crust of bread in his mouth, with one end of it out of his lips. Down they came like bees at a flower, and flew off with it crumb by crumb.

9. When they thought he slept too long **in** the morning, **they would fly** in and sit

on the bedpost, and call him up with their chirp.

10. They went with him to church, and while he said his prayers and sang his hymns in it, they sat in the trees, and sang their praises to the same good God who cares for them as he does for us.

11. Thus the love and trust of birds were a joy to him all his life long; and such love and trust no boy or girl can fail to win with the same kind heart, voice, and eye that he had.

Adapted from Elihu Burritt.

LESSON XVII.

WHAT THE MINUTES SAY.

1. We are but minutes—little things!
   Each one furnished with sixty wings,
   With which we fly on our unseen track,
   And not a minute ever comes back.

2. We are but minutes; use us well,
   For how we are used we must one day tell.
   Who uses minutes, has hours to use;
   Who loses minutes, whole years must lose.

LESSON XVIII.

dīed	wǒm′an	eon vĭnçed′	a māzed′	wrōte
pĭt′y	mis tāke′	re wạrd′ed	ḡrāte′fụl	chĕck

dis trĕss′	hĕṣ i tā′tion
hŭṣ′band	mu ṣĭ′cian
wĭd′ow	as sĭst′ançe

THE WIDOW AND THE MERCHANT.

1. A merchant, who was very fond of music, was asked by a poor widow to give her some assistance. Her husband, who was a musician, had died, and left her very poor indeed.

2. The merchant saw that the widow and her daughter, who was with her, were in great

distress. He looked with pity into their pale faces, and was convinced by their conduct that their sad story was true.

3. "How much do you want, my good woman?" said the merchant.

4. "Five dollars will save us," said the poor widow, with some hesitation.

5. The merchant sat down at his desk, took a piece of paper, wrote a few lines on it, and gave it to the widow with the words, "Take it to the bank you see on the other side of the street."

6. The grateful widow and her daughter, without stopping to read the note, hastened to the bank. The banker at once counted out fifty dollars instead of five, and passed them to the widow.

7. She was amazed when she saw so much money. "Sir, there is a mistake here," she said. "You have given me fifty dollars, and I asked for only five."

8. The banker looked at the note once more, and said, "The check calls for fifty dollars."

9. "It is a mistake—indeed it is," said the widow.

10. The banker then asked her to wait

a few minutes, while he went to see the merchant who gave her the note.

11. "Yes," said the merchant, when he had heard the banker's story, "I did make a mistake. I wrote fifty instead of five hundred. Give the poor widow five hundred dollars, for such honesty is poorly rewarded with even that sum."

LESSON XIX.

| wīreş | trāde | bär′gain | săd′ness | prĭş′on erş |
| war | Frĕnch | a piēçe′ | nŭm′ber | re şŏlved′ |

THE BIRDS SET FREE.

1. A man was walking one day through a large city. On a street corner he saw a boy with a number of small birds for sale, in a cage.

2. He looked with sadness upon the little prisoners flying about the cage, peeping through the wires, beating them with their wings, and trying to get out.

3. He stood for some time looking at the birds. At last he said to the boy, "How much do you ask for your birds?"

4. "Fifty cents apiece, sir," said the boy. "I do not mean how much apiece," said the man, "but how much for all of them? I want to buy them *all*."

5. The boy began to count, and found they came to five dollars. "There is your money,"

said the man. The boy took it, well pleased with his morning's trade.

6. No sooner was the bargain settled than the man opened the cage door, and let all the birds fly away.

7. The boy, in great surprise, cried, "What did you do that for, sir? You have lost all your birds."

8. "I will tell you why I did it," said the man. "I was shut up three years in a French prison, as a prisoner of war, and I am resolved never to see anything in prison which I can make free."

LESSON XX.

down'y   fĭrm'ly   stāid   pĕt'alṣ   erīme

A MOMENT TOO LATE.

1. A moment too late, my beautiful bird,
    A moment too late are you now;
The wind has your soft, downy nest disturbed —
    The nest that you hung on the bough.

2. A moment too late; that string in your bill,
    Would have fastened it firmly and strong;
But see, there it goes, rolling over the hill!
    Oh, you staid a moment too long.

3. A moment, one moment too late, busy bee;
    The honey has dropped from the flower:
No use to creep under the petals and see;
    It stood ready to drop for an hour.

4. A moment too late; had you sped on your wing,
    The honey would not have been gone;

Now you see what a very, a very sad thing
    'T is to stay a moment too long.

5. Little girl, never be a moment too late,
    It will soon end in trouble or crime;
Better be an hour early, and stand and wait,
    Than a moment behind the time.

6. If the bird and the bee, little boy, were too late,
    Remember, as you play along
On your way to school, with pencil and slate,
    Never stay a moment too long.

LESSON XXI.

Wĕst In'dĭeş	a dôrn'	ap prōach'	mō'tion	at tăched'
sụḡ'ar plŭm	eŏt'ton	ĭn'stĭnet	ŏb'ject	de fĕnd'ing
nĕç'es sa ry	răp'id	brĭl'liant	fī'berş	se vēre'ly

HUMMING BIRDS.

1. The most beautiful humming birds are found in the West Indies and South America. The crest of the tiny head of one of these shines like a sparkling crown of colored light.

2. The shades of color that adorn its breast, are equally brilliant. As the bird

flits from one object to another, it looks more like a bright flash of sunlight than it does like a living being.

3. But, you ask, why are they called humming birds? It is because they make a soft, humming noise by the rapid motion of their wings—a motion so rapid, that as they fly you can only see that they have wings.

4. One day when walking in the woods, I found the nest of one of the smallest humming birds. It was about half the size of a very small hen's egg, and

was attached to a twig no thicker than a steel knitting needle.

5. It seemed to have been made of cotton fibers, and was covered with the softest bits of leaf and bark. It had two eggs in it, quite white, and each about as large as a small sugarplum.

6. When you approach the spot where one of these birds has built its nest, it is necessary to be careful. The mother bird will dart at you and try to peck your eyes. Its sharp beak may hurt your eyes most severely, and even destroy the sight.

7. The poor little thing knows no other way of defending its young, and instinct teaches it that you might carry off its nest if you could find it.

LESSON XXII.

de çīde′	bŭe′kled	moun′tain	shĕl′ter	pär′ty
dis pūte′	sue çeed′	fōr′çi bly	măn′tle	ȯv′en

THE WIND AND THE SUN.

A FABLE.

1. A dispute once arose between the Wind and the Sun, as to which was the stronger.

2. To decide the matter, they agreed to try their power on a traveler. That party which should first strip him of his cloak, was to win the day.

3. The Wind began. He blew a cutting blast, which tore up the mountain oaks by their roots, and made the whole forest look like a wreck.

4. But the traveler, though at first he could scarcely keep his cloak on his back, ran under a hill for shelter, and buckled his mantle about him more closely.

5. The Wind having thus tried his utmost power in vain, the Sun began.

6. Bursting through a thick cloud, he darted his sultry beams so forcibly upon the traveler's head, that the poor fellow was almost melted.

7. "This," said he, "is past all bearing. It is so hot, that one might as well be in an oven."

8. So he quickly threw off his cloak, and went into the shade of a tree to cool himself.

9. This fable teaches us, that gentle means will often succeed where forcible ones will fail.

LESSON XXIII.

sĭnk'ing strēam'let sweet'ness eow'slĭp

SUNSET.

Now the sun is sinking
 In the golden west;
Birds and bees and children
 All have gone to rest;

And the merry streamlet,
　As it runs along,
With a voice of sweetness
　Sings its evening song.

2.

Cowslip, daisy, violet,
　In their little beds,
All among the grasses
　Hide their heavy heads;
There they'll all, sweet darlings,
　Lie in the happy dreams.
Till the rosy morning
　Wakes them with its beams.

LESSON XXIV.

o pĭn'ion　　pĭ ȧn'o　　eōarse　　bāthe　　sweep

BEAUTIFUL HANDS.

1. "O Miss Roberts! what coarse-looking hands Mary Jessup has!" said Daisy Marvin, as she walked home from school with her teacher.

2. "In my opinion, Daisy, Mary's hands are the prettiest in the class."

3. "Why, Miss Roberts, they are as red and hard as they can be. How they would look if she were to try to play on a piano!" exclaimed Daisy.

4. Miss Roberts took Daisy's hands in hers, and said, "Your hands are very soft and white, Daisy—just the hands to look beautiful on a piano; yet they lack one beauty that Mary's hands have. Shall I tell you what the difference is?"

5. "Yes, please, Miss Roberts."

6. "Well, Daisy, Mary's hands are always busy. They wash dishes; they make fires; they hang out clothes, and help to wash them, too; they sweep, and dust, and sew; they are always trying to help her poor, hard-working mother.

7. "Besides, they wash and dress the children; they mend their toys and dress their dolls; yet, they find time to bathe the head of the little girl who is so sick in the next house to theirs.

8. "They are full of good deeds to every living thing. I have seen them patting the **tired horse and the lame dog in the street.**

They are always ready to help those who
need help."

9. "I shall never think Mary's hands are
ugly any more, Miss Roberts."

10. "I am glad to hear you say that,
Daisy; and I must tell you that they are
beautiful because they do their work gladly
and cheerfully."

11. "O Miss Roberts! I feel so ashamed
of myself, and so sorry," said Daisy, looking
into her teacher's face with tearful eyes.

12. " Then, my dear, show your sorrow by deeds of kindness. The good alone are really beautiful."

LESSON XXV.

a void'	pre vĕnt'	for gīve'	rīṣe	gūīde
dūr'ing	pout'ing	pro tĕe'tion	slăm	măn'ner
pee'vish	howl'ing	săt'is fīed	trŭst	ăṇ'gry

THINGS TO REMEMBER.

1. When you rise in the morning, remember who kept you from danger during the hight. Remember who watched over you while you slept, and whose sun shines around you, and gives you the sweet light of day.

2. Let God have the thanks of your heart, for his kindness and his care; and pray for his protection during the wakeful hours of day.

3. Remember that God made all creatures to be happy, and will do nothing that may prevent their being so, without good reason for it.

4. When you are at the table, do not eat in a greedy manner, like a pig. Eat quietly,

3. 5

and do not reach forth your hand for the food, but ask some one to help you.

5. Do not become peevish and pout, because you do not get a part of everything. Be satisfied with what is given you.

6. Avoid a pouting face, angry looks, and angry words. Do not slam the doors. Go quietly up and down stairs; and never make a loud noise about the house.

7. Be kind and gentle in your manners; not like the howling winter storm, but like the bright summer morning.

8. Do always as your parents bid you. Obey them with a ready mind, and with a pleasant face.

9. Never do anything that you would be afraid or ashamed that your parents should know. Remember, if no one else sees you, God does, from whom you can not hide even your most secret thought.

10. At night, before you go to sleep, think whether you have done anything that was wrong during the day, and pray to God to forgive you. If any one has done you wrong, forgive him in your heart.

11. If you have not learned something useful, or been in some way useful, during

the past day, think that it is a day lost,
and be very sorry for it.

12. Trust in the Lord, and He will guide
you in the way of good men. The path of
the just is as the shining light that shineth
more and more unto the perfect day.

13. We must do all the good we can to
all men, for this is well pleasing in the
sight of God. He delights to see his children walk in love, and do good one to
another.

LESSON XXVI.

ex ăet'ly	fōld'ing	cheeşe	chăm'ber	răt'tling
pro trŭd'ed	fōre'pạwş	ḡāzed	doubt	re lēased'
per plĕxed'	lăt'tĭçe	queer	eō'zy	stâir'eāse

THREE LITTLE MICE.

1. I will tell you the story of three little mice,
    If you will keep still and listen to me,
Who live in a cage that is cozy and nice,
    And are just as cunning as cunning can be.
They look very wise, with their pretty red eyes,
    That seem just exactly like little round beads;
They are white as the snow, and stand up in a row
    Whenever we do not attend to their needs;—

2. Stand up in a row in a comical way,—
　　Now folding their forepaws as if saying,
　　　"please;"
　Now rattling the lattice, as much as to say,
　　"We shall not stay here without more bread
　　　and cheese."
　They are not at all shy, as you'll find, if you try
　　To make them run up in their chamber to bed;
　If they do n't want to go, why, they won't go—
　　　ah! no,
　　Though you tap with your finger each queer
　　　little head.

3. One day as I stood by the side of the cage,
　　Through the bars there protruded a funny,
　　　round tail;

Just for mischief I caught it, and soon, in a rage,
　Its owner set up a most pitiful wail.
He looked in dismay,—there was something to
　　　pay,—
　But what was the matter he could not make out;
What was holding him so, when he wanted to go
　To see what his brothers upstairs were about?

4. But soon from the chamber the others rushed
　　　down,
　Impatient to learn what the trouble might be;
I have not a doubt that each brow wore a frown,
　Only frowns on their brows are not easy to see.
For a moment they gazed, perplexed and amazed;
　Then began both together to—gnaw off the tail!
So, quick I released him,— do you think that it
　　　pleased him?
　And up the small staircase they fled like a gale.

Julia C. R. Dorr.

LESSON XXVII.

Ed'ward	re çeive'	wrĕtch'ed	thou'şand	ḡrăt'i tūde
re pēat'	lăn'ḡuaġe	shĭv'er ing	Gēr'man	ŭn der stŏŏd'

THE NEW YEAR.

1. One pleasant New-year morning, Edward rose, and washed and dressed himself

in haste. He wanted to be first to wish a happy New Year.

2. He looked in every room, and shouted the words of welcome. He ran into the

street, to repeat them to those he might meet.

3. When he came back, his father gave him two bright, new silver dollars.

4. His face lighted up as he took them. He had wished for a long time to buy some pretty books that he had seen at the bookstore.

5. He left the house with a light heart, intending to buy the books.

6. As he ran down the street, he saw a poor German family, the father, mother, and three children shivering with cold.

7. "I wish you a happy New Year," said Edward, as he was gayly passing on. The man shook his head.

8. "You do not belong to this country," said Edward. The man again shook his head, for he could not understand or speak our language.

9. But he pointed to his mouth, and to the children, as if to say, "These little ones have had nothing to eat for a long time."

10. Edward quickly understood that these poor people were in distress. He took out his dollars, and gave one to the man, and the other to his wife.

11. How their eyes sparkled with gratitude! They said something in their language, which doubtless meant, "We thank you a thousand times, and will remember you in our prayers."

12. When Edward came home, his father asked what books he had bought. He hung his head a moment, but quickly looked up.

13. "I have bought no books," said he, "I gave my money to some poor people, who seemed to be very hungry and wretched.

14. "I think I can wait for my books till next New Year. Oh, if you had seen how glad they were to receive the money!"

15. "My dear boy," said his father, "here is a whole bundle of books. I give them to you, more as a reward for your goodness of heart than as a New-year gift.

16. "I saw you give the money to the poor German family. It was no small sum for a little boy to give cheerfully.

17. "Be thus ever ready to help the poor, and wretched, and distressed; and every year of your life will be to you a happy New Year."

LESSON XXVIII.

| stŏck | spĭr'it | hŭm'ble | glōōm'y | sŭn'dī al |
| fŏl'ly | stee'ple | stū'pid | bōast'ing | mŏd'es ty |

THE CLOCK AND THE SUNDIAL.

A FABLE.

1. One gloomy day, the clock on a church steeple, looking down on a sundial, said,

"How stupid it is in you to stand there all the while like a stock!

2. "You never tell the hour till a bright sun looks forth from the sky, and gives you leave. I go merrily round, day and night, in summer and winter the same, without asking his leave.

3. "I tell the people the time to rise, to go to dinner, and to come to church.

4. "Hark! I am going to strike now; one, two, three, four. There it is for you. How silly you look! You can say nothing."

5. The sun, at that moment, broke forth from behind a cloud, and showed, by the sundial, that the clock was half an hour behind the right time.

6. The boasting clock now held his tongue, and the dial only smiled at his folly.

7. MORAL.—Humble modesty is more often right than a proud and boasting spirit.

LESSON XXIX.

pŭn′ish ăe′tionṣ wĭck′ed fạlse′hŏŏd wāke′fụl

REMEMBER.

1. Remember, child, remember,
   That God is in the sky;
   That He looks down on all we do,
   With an ever-wakeful eye.

2. Remember, oh remember,
   That, all the day and night,
   He sees our thoughts and actions
   With an ever-watchful sight.

3. Remember, child, remember,
    That God is good and true;
That He wishes us to always be
    Like Him in all we do.

4. Remember that He ever hates
    A falsehood or a lie;
Remember He will punish, too,
    The wicked, by and by.

5. Remember, oh remember,
    That He is like a friend,
And wishes us to holy be,
    And happy, in the end.

6. Remember, child, remember,
    To pray to Him in heaven;
And if you have been doing wrong,
    Oh, ask to be forgiven.

7. Be sorry, in your little prayer,
    And whisper in his ear;
Ask his forgiveness and his love,
    And He will surely hear.

8. Remember, child, remember,
    That you love, with all your might,

The God who watches o'er us,
   And gives us each delight;
Who guards us ever through the day,
   And saves us in the night.

LESSON XXX.

dēal	strāight	eoŭr'aġe	re prōach'	eow'ard ĭçe
dĕpth	ĕf'fŏrt	eow'ard	de ṣẽrved'	sehōōl'mātes

COURAGE AND COWARDICE.

1. Robert and Henry were going home from school, when, on turning a corner, Robert cried out, "A fight! let us go and see!"

2. "No," said Henry; "let us go quietly home and not meddle with this quarrel. We have nothing to do with it, and may get into mischief."

3. "You are a coward, and afraid to go," said Robert, and off he ran. Henry went straight home, and in the afternoon went to school, as usual.

4. But Robert had told all the boys that Henry was a coward, and they laughed at him a great deal.

5. Henry had learned, however, that true courage is shown most in bearing reproach when not deserved, and that he ought to be afraid of nothing but doing wrong.

6. A few days after, Robert was bathing with some schoolmates, and got out of his depth. He struggled, and screamed for help, but all in vain.

7. The boys who had called Henry a coward, got out of the water as fast as they could, but they did not even try to help him.

8. Robert was fast sinking, when Henry threw off his clothes, and sprang into the water. He reached Robert just as he was sinking the last time.

9. By great effort, and with much danger to himself, he brought Robert to the shore, and thus saved his life.

10. Robert and his schoolmates were ashamed at having called Henry a coward. They owned that he had more courage than any of them.

11. Never be afraid to do good, but always fear to do evil.

LESSON XXXI.

ēast'ern	de lĭv'er ançe	wĕight	fā'vor ĭte	ĕlĕv'er
sāil'or	e nôr'moŭs	eōurt	quạn'ti ty	sŭb'jeet
ex pĕnse'	ĕl'e phant	strōked	ma çhïne'	lēan'ing
ō'pen ing	dĭf'fi eul ty	rĭṣ'en	re liēved'	ĕmp'ty

WEIGHING AN ELEPHANT.

1. "An eastern king," said Teddy's mother, "had been saved from some great danger. To show his gratitude for deliverance, he vowed he would give to the poor the weight of his favorite elephant in silver."

2. "Oh! what a great quantity that would be," cried Lily, opening her eyes very wide. "But how *could* you weigh an elephant?"

asked Teddy, who was a quiet, thoughtful boy.

3. "There was the difficulty," said his mother. "The wise and learned men of the court stroked their long beards, and talked the matter over, but no one found out how to weigh the elephant.

4. "At last, a poor old sailor found safe and simple means by which to weigh the enormous beast. The thousands and thousands of pieces of silver were counted out to the people; and crowds of the poor were relieved by the clever thought of the sailor."

5. "O mamma," said Lily, "do tell us what it was!"

6. "Stop, stop!" said Teddy. "I want to think for myself—think hard—and find out how an elephant's weight could be known, with little trouble and expense."

7. "I am well pleased," said his mother, "that my little boy should set his mind to work on the subject. If he can find out the sailor's secret before night, he shall have that orange for his pains."

8. The boy thought hard and long. Lily laughed at her brother's grave looks, as he sat leaning his head on his hands. Often

she teased him with the question, "Can you weigh an elephant, Teddy?"

9. At last, while eating his supper, Teddy suddenly cried out, "I have it now!"

10. "Do you think so?" asked his mother.

11. "How would you do it," asked Lily.

12. "First, I would have a big boat brought very close to the shore, and would have planks laid across, so that the elephant could walk right into it."

13. "Oh, such a great, heavy beast would make it sink low in the water," said Lily.

14. "Of course it would," said her brother. "Then I would mark on the outside of the boat the exact height to which the water had risen all around it while the elephant was inside. Then he should march on shore, leaving the boat quite empty."

15. "But I don't see the use of all this," said Lily.

16. "Don't you?" cried Teddy, in surprise. "Why, I should then bring the heaps of silver, and throw them into the boat till their weight would sink it to the mark made by the elephant. That would show that the weight of each was the same."

17. "How funny!" cried Lily; "you would make a weighing machine of the boat?"

18. "That is my plan," said Teddy.

19. "That was the sailor's plan," said his mother. "You have earned the orange, my boy;" and she gave it to him with a smile.

Adapted from A. L. O. E.

3, 6.

LESSON XXXII.

răṇks	glō'ry	ar rāyed'	wĕap'onṣ	lĭv'ing
elăd	är'mor	vĭe'to ry	eŏn'test	băt'tle
blôod	en lĭst'	mŭs'tered	lŏng'ing	wạr'rior

THE SOLDIER.

1. A soldier! a soldier! I'm longing to be:
   The name and the life of a soldier for me!
   I would not be living at ease and at play;
   True honor and glory I'd win in my day.

2. A soldier! a soldier! in armor arrayed;
   My weapons in hand, of no contest afraid;
   I'd ever be ready to strike the first blow,
   And to fight my way through the ranks of the foe.

3. But then, let me tell you, no blood would I shed,
   No victory seek o'er the dying and dead;
   A far braver soldier than this would I be;
   A warrior of Truth, in the ranks of the free.

4. A soldier! a soldier! Oh, then, let me be!
   My friends, I invite you, enlist now with me.
   Truth's bands shall be mustered, love's foes shall
           give way!
   Let's up, and be clad in our battle array!

                                        J. G. Adams.

LESSON XXXIII.

thĭck'et	härsh'ly	wräth	whĕnçe	răm'bling
prọv'ing	tō'ward	ĕeh'o	mŏck'ing	ăn'g̅ri ly
fōōl'ish	a broạd'	erŏss	Bī'ble	ĭn'stant ly

THE ECHO.

1. As Robert was one day rambling about, he happened to cry out, "Ho, ho!" He instantly heard coming back from a hill near by, the same words, "Ho, ho!"

2. In great surprise, he said with a loud voice, "Who are you?" Upon this, the same words came back, "Who are you?"

3. Robert now cried out harshly, "You must be a very foolish fellow." "Foolish fellow!" came back from the hill.

4. Robert became angry, and with loud and fierce words went toward the spot whence the sounds came. The words all came back to him in the same angry tone.

5. He then went into the thicket, and looked for the boy who, as he thought, was mocking him; but he could find nobody anywhere.

6. When he went home, he told his moth-

er that some boy had hid himself in the wood, for the purpose of mocking him.

7. "Robert," said his mother, "you are angry with yourself alone. You heard nothing but your own words."

8. "Why, mother, how can that be?" said Robert. "Did you never hear an echo?" asked his mother. "An echo, dear mother? No, ma'am. What is it?"

9. "I will tell you," said his mother. "You know, when you play with your ball,

and throw it against the side of a house, it bounds back to you." "Yes, mother," said he, "and I catch it again."

10. "Well," said his mother, "if I were in the open air, by the side of a hill or a large barn, and should speak very loud, my voice would be sent back, so that I could hear again the very words which I spoke.

11. "That, my son, is an echo. When you thought some one was mocking you, it was only the hill before you, echoing, or sending back, your own voice.

12. "The bad boy, as you thought it was, spoke no more angrily than yourself. If you had spoken kindly, you would have heard a kind reply.

13. "Had you spoken in a low, sweet, gentle tone, the voice that came back would have been as low, sweet, and gentle as your own.

14. "The Bible says, 'A soft answer turneth away wrath.' Remember this when you are at play with your schoolmates.

15. "If any of them should be offended, and speak in a loud, angry tone, remember the echo, and let your words be soft and kind.

16. "When you come home from school, and find your little brother cross and peevish, speak mildly to him. You will soon see a smile on his lips, and find that his tones will become mild and sweet.

17. "Whether you are in the fields or in the woods, at school or at play, at home or abroad, remember,

> The good and the kind,
> By kindness their love ever proving,
> Will dwell with the pure and the loving."

LESSON XXXIV.

fāint	eol lĕet′	re frĕsh′	līn′ing	hăp′pi ness
fēast	seär′let	ŏf′fered	lĭft′ing	straw′ber rieş

GEORGE'S FEAST.

1. George's mother was very poor. Instead of having bright, blazing fires in winter, she had nothing to burn but dry sticks, which George picked up from under the trees and hedges.

2. One fine day in July, she sent George to the woods, which were about two miles from the village in which she lived. He

was to stay there all day, to get as much wood as he could collect.

3. It was a bright, sunny day, and George worked very hard; so that by the time the

sun was high, he was hot, and wished for a cool place where he might rest and eat his dinner.

4. While he hunted about the bank, he saw among the moss some fine, wild straw-berries, which were a bright scarlet with ripeness.

5. "How good these will be with my bread and butter!" thought George; and lining his little cap with leaves, he set to work eagerly to gather all he could find, and then seated himself by the brook.

6. It was a pleasant place, and George felt happy and contented. He thought how much his mother would like to see him there, and to be there herself, instead of in her dark, close room in the village.

7. George thought of all this, and just as he was lifting the first strawberry to his mouth, he said to himself, "How much mother would like these;" and he stopped, and put the strawberry back again.

8. "Shall I save them for her?" said he, thinking how much they would refresh her, yet still looking at them with a longing eye.

9. "I will eat half, and take the other half to her," said he at last; and he divided them into two heaps. But each heap looked so small, that he put them together again.

10. "I will only taste one," thought he; but, as he again lifted it to his mouth, he saw that he had taken the finest, and he put it back. "I will keep them all for her,"

said he, and he covered them up nicely, till he should go home.

11. When the sun was beginning to sink, George set out for home. How happy he felt, then, that he had all his strawberries for his sick mother. The nearer he came to his home, the less he wished to taste them.

12. Just as he had thrown down his wood, he heard his mother's faint voice calling him from the next room. "Is that you, George? I am glad you have come, for I am thirsty, and am longing for some tea."

13. George ran in to her, and joyfully offered his wild strawberries. "And you saved them for your sick mother, did you?" said she, laying her hand fondly on his head, while the tears stood in her eyes. "God will bless you for all this, my child."

14. Could the eating of the strawberries have given George half the happiness he felt at this moment?

LEON CUIPON.

LESSON XXXV.

hăl'low	ā mĕn'	temp tā'tion	ḡrā' cioŭs
kĭng'dòm	for ḡĭve'	trans ḡrĕs'sionş	sup plīed'
pōr'tion	boun'ty	wēak'ness	hĕlp'less
dẹign	sŏl'emn	eom păs'sion	plūm'ȧġe
re vēre'	se eūre'	for ĕv'er	pär'donş

THE LORD'S PRAYER.

1. Our Father in heaven,
    We hallow thy name;
  May thy kingdom holy
    On earth be the same;
  Oh, give to us daily
    Our portion of bread;
  It is from thy bounty,
    That all must be fed.

2. Forgive our transgressions,
    And teach us to know
  The humble compassion
    That pardons each foe;
  Keep us from temptation,
    From weakness and sin,
  And thine be the glory
    Forever! Amen!

AN EVENING PRAYER.

I.

Before I close my eyes in sleep,
  Lord, hear my evening prayer,
And deign a helpless child to keep,
  With thy protecting care.

2.

Though young in years, I have been taught
  Thy name to love and fear;
Of thee to think with solemn thought;
  Thy goodness to revere.

3.

That goodness gives each simple flower
  Its scent and beauty, too;
And feeds it in night's darkest hour
  With heaven's refreshing dew.

4.

The little birds that sing all day
  In many a leafy wood,
By thee are clothed in plumage gay,
  By thee supplied with food.

5.

And when at night they cease to sing,
By thee protected still,
Their young ones sleep beneath their wing,
Secure from every ill.

6.

Thus mayst thou guard with gracious arm
The bed whereon I lie,
And keep a child from every harm
By thine own watchful eye.

Bernard Barton

LESSON XXXVI.

pos sĕs'sion	tôr'ment	suḡ ḡĕst'ed	ob s̱ērved'
săt is făe'tion	thiĕf	an̲x ī'e ty	fī'nal ly
bur'y ing (bĕr'-)	eŏn'scioŭs	erĭt'ie al	brĕath'less
ex pē'ri ençed	re spŏnse'	ĕv'i dent	ĭn ter fēred'

FINDING THE OWNER.

1. "It 's mine," said Fred, showing a white-handled pocketknife, with every blade perfect and shining. "Just what I 've always

wanted." And he turned the prize over and over with evident satisfaction.

2. "I guess I know who owns it," said Tom, looking at it with a critical eye.

3. "I guess you do n't," was the quick response. "It is n't Mr. Raymond's," said Fred, shooting wide of the mark.

4. "I know that; Mr. Raymond's is twice as large," observed Tom, going on with his drawing lesson.

5. Do you suppose Fred took any comfort in that knife? Not a bit of comfort did he take. He was conscious all the time of having something in his possession that did

not belong to him; and Tom's suspicion interfered sadly with his enjoyment.

6. Finally, it became such a torment to him, that he had serious thoughts of burning it, or burying it, or giving it away; but a better plan suggested itself.

7. "Tom," said he, one day at recess, "did n't you say you thought you knew who owned that knife I found?"

8. "Yes, I did; it looked like Doctor Perry's." And Tom ran off to his play, without giving the knife another thought.

9. Dr. Perry's! Why, Fred would have time to go to the doctor's office before recess closed: so he started in haste, and found the old gentleman getting ready to visit a patient. "Is this yours?" cried Fred, in breathless haste, holding up the cause of a week's anxiety.

10. "It was," said the doctor; "but I lost it the other day."

11. "I found it," said Fred, "and have felt like a thief ever since. Here, take it; I 've got to run."

12. "Hold on!" said the doctor. "I 've got a new one, and you are quite welcome to this."

13. "Am I? May I? Oh! thank you!" And with what a different feeling he kept it from that which he had experienced for a week!

LESSON XXXVII.

im mē'di ate ly

ehăr'ae ter

squēal

snăpped

shŭnned

quĭllṣ

tĕr'ri bly

erĕv'iç eṣ

en eoun'tered

pre pâred'

pŏl'i çy

prowl'ing

doŭ'ble

ĭn'seet

de vour

es eāpe

frāme'wõrk   nīght'mâre   dis ḡŭst'ing   quạd'rụ ped

BATS.

1. Bats are very strange little animals, having hair like mice, and wings like birds. During the day, they live in crevices of rocks, in caves, and in other dark places.

2. At night, they go forth in search of food; and, no doubt, you have seen them fly-

ing about, catching such insects as happen to be out rather late at night.

3. The wings of a bat have no quills. They are only thin pieces of skin stretched upon a framework of bones. Besides this, it may be said that while he is a quadruped, he can rise into the air and fly from place to place like a bird.

4. There is a funny fable about the bat, founded upon this double character of beast and bird, which I will tell you.

5. An owl was once prowling about, when he came across a bat. So he caught him in his claws, and was about to devour him. Upon this, the bat began to squeal terribly; and he said to the owl, "Pray, what do you take me for, that you use me thus?"

6. "Why, you are a bird, to be sure," said the owl, "and I am fond of birds. I love dearly to break their little bones."

7. "Well," said the bat, "I thought there was some mistake. I am no bird. Don't you see, Mr. Owl, that I have no feathers, and that I am covered with hair like a mouse?"

8. "Sure enough," said the owl, in great surprise; "I see it now. Really, I took **you**

for a bird, but it appears you are only a kind
of mouse. I ate a mouse last night, and it
gave me the nightmare. I can't bear mice!
Bah! it makes me sick to think of it." So
the owl let the bat go.

9. The very next night, the bat encoun-
tered another danger. He was snapped up
by puss, who took him for a mouse, and immediately prepared to eat him.

10. "I beg you to stop one moment," said
the bat. "Pray, Miss Puss, what do you
suppose I am?" "A mouse, to be sure!"
said the cat. "Not at all," said the bat,
spreading his long wings.

11. "Sure enough," said the cat: "you
seem to be a bird, though your feathers are

3, 7.

not very fine. I eat birds sometimes, but I am tired of them just now, having lately devoured four young robins; so you may go. But, bird or mouse, it will be your best policy to keep out of my way hereafter."

12. The meaning of this fable is, that a person playing a double part may sometimes escape danger; but he is always, like the bat, a creature that is disgusting to everybody, and shunned by all.

S. G. Goodrich—Adapted.

LESSON XXXVIII.

tĭnts	shēaveş	fīre′flīes	chĭm′ney	tĭn̮′kle
lạwnş	whīrl	bŭt′ter ĕŭp	lōw′ing	lánçe

A SUMMER DAY.

1. This is the way the morning dawns:
    Rosy tints on flowers and trees,
    Winds that wake the birds and bees,
   Dewdrops on the fields and lawns—
   This is the way the morning dawns.

2. This is the way the sun comes up:
    Gold on brook and glossy leaves,

Mist that melts above the sheaves,
Vine, and rose, and buttercup—
This is the way the sun comes up.

3. This is the way the river flows:
  Here a whirl, and there a dance;
  Slowly now, then, like a lance,
 Swiftly to the sea it goes—
 This is the way the river flows.

4. This is the way the rain comes down:
    Tinkle, tinkle, drop by drop,
    Over roof and chimney top;
  Boughs that bend, and skies that frown—
  This is the way the rain comes down.

5. This is the way the birdie sings:
    "Baby birdies in the nest,
    You I surely love the best;
  Over you I fold my wings"—
  This is the way the birdie sings.

6. This is the way the daylight dies:
    Cows are lowing in the lane,
    Fireflies wink on hill and plain;
  Yellow, red, and purple skies—
  This is the way the daylight dies.

George Cooper.

LESSON XXXIX.

çhăn de liēr′	Pï′şa	Lȯn′dȯn	Fēr′ġu son
pōr′traits	I′şaae	in vĕn′tion	Găl i lē′o
pĕn′du lŭm	ĕn′ġĭne	whāle′bōne	lĕe′tureş
lō eo mō′tĭve	mŏt′to	Eng′land (ĭn′gland)	tēa′kĕt tle
dis eȯv′ered	swāy′ing	dis eoŭr′aġed	im prọved′

I WILL THINK OF IT.

1. " I will think of it." It is easy to say this; but do you know what great things have come from thinking?

2. We can not see our thoughts, or hear, or taste, or feel them; and yet what mighty power they have!

3. Sir Isaac Newton was seated in his garden on a summer's evening, when he saw an apple fall from a tree. He began to *think*, and, in trying to find out why the apple fell, discovered how the earth, sun, moon, and stars are kept ·in their places.

4. A boy named James Watt sat quietly by the fireside, watching the lid of the tea-kettle as it moved up and down. He began to *think;* he wanted to find out why the steam in the kettle moved the heavy lid.

5. From that time he went on thinking, and thinking; and when he became a man, he improved the steam engine so much that it could, with the greatest ease, do the work of many horses.

6. When you see a steamboat, a steam mill, or a locomotive, remember that it would never have been built if it had not been for the hard thinking of some one.

7. A man named Galileo was once standing in the cathedral of Pisa, when he saw a chandelier swaying to and fro.

8. This set him *thinking*, and it led to the invention of the pendulum.

9. James Ferguson was a poor Scotch shepherd boy. Once, seeing the inside of a watch, he was filled with wonder. "Why should I not make a watch?" thought he.

10. But how was he to get the materials out of which to make the wheels and the mainspring? He soon found how to get them: he made the mainspring out of a piece of whalebone. He then made a wooden clock which kept good time.

11. He began, also, to copy pictures with a pen, and portraits with oil colors. In a few years, while still a small boy, he earned money enough to support his father.

12. When he became a man, he went to London to live. Some of the wisest men in England, and the king himself, used to attend his lectures. His motto was, "I will think of it;" and he made his thoughts useful to himself and the world.

13. Boys, when you have a difficult lesson to learn, don't feel discouraged, and ask some one to help you before helping yourselves. Think, and by thinking you will learn how to think to some purpose.

LESSON XL.

CHARLIE AND ROB.

1. "Don't you hate splitting wood?" asked Charlie, as he sat down on a log to hinder Rob for a while.

2. "No, I rather like it. When I get hold of a tough old fellow, I say, 'See here, now, you think you're the stronger, and are going to beat me; so I'll split you up into kindling wood.'"

3. "Pshaw!" said Charlie, laughing; "and it's only a stick of wood."

4. "Yes; but you see I pretend it's a lesson, or a tough job of any kind, and it's nice to conquer it."

5. "I don't want to conquer such things; I don't care what becomes of them. I wish I were a man, and a rich one."

6. "Well, Charlie, if you live long enough you'll be a man, without wishing for it; and as for the rich part, I mean to be that myself."

7. "You do. How do you expect to get your money? By sawing wood?"

8. "May be—some of it; that's as good a

way as any, so long as it lasts. I do n't care
how I get rich, you know, so that it's in an
honest and useful way."

9. "I'd like to sleep over the next ten
years, and wake up to find myself a young
man with a splendid education and plenty of
money."

10. "Humph! I am not sleepy—a night at a time is enough for me. I mean to work the next ten years. You see there are things that you've got to *work* out—you can't *sleep* them out."

11. "I hate work," said Charlie, "that is, such work as sawing and splitting wood, and doing chores. I'd like to do some big work, like being a clerk in a bank or something of that sort."

12. "Wood has to be sawed and split before it can be burned," said Rob. "I don't know but I'll be a clerk in a bank some time; I'm working towards it. I'm keeping father's accounts for him."

13. How Charlie laughed! "I should think that was a long way from being a bank clerk. I suppose your father sells two tables and six chairs, some days, doesn't he?"

14. "Sometimes more than that, and sometimes not so much," said Rob, in perfect good humor.

15. "I didn't say I was a bank clerk now. I said I was working towards it. Am I not nearer it by keeping a little bit of a book than I should be if I didn't keep any book at all?"

16. "Not a whit — such things *happen,*" said Charlie, as he started to go.

17. Now, which of these boys, do you think, grew up to be a rich and useful man, and which of them joined a party of tramps before he was thirty years old?

DEFINITIONS.—1. Hĭn'der, *interrupt, prevent from working.* 4. Cŏn'quer, *overcome, master.* 9. Splĕn'did, *very fine, complete.* Ed u eā'tion, *acquired knowledge.* 11. Chōreş, *the light work about a house or yard.*

LESSON XLI.

RAY AND HIS KITE.

1. Ray was thought to be an odd boy. You will think him so, too, when you have read this story.

2. Ray liked well enough to play with the boys at school; yet he liked better to be alone under the shade of some tree, reading a fairy tale or dreaming daydreams. But there was one sport that he liked as well as his companions; that was kiteflying.

3. One day when he was flying his kite, he said to himself, "I wonder if anybody ever tried to fly a kite at night. It seems

to me it would be nice. But then, if it
were very dark, the kite could not be seen.
What if I should fasten a light to it, though?
That would make
it show. I'll try it
this very night."

4. As soon as it
was dark, without

saying a word to
anybody, he took
his kite and lan-
tern, and went to
a large, open lot,
about a quarter of
a mile from his
home. "Well,"
thought he, "this
is queer. How
lonely and still it seems without any other
boys around! But I am going to fly my
kite, anyway."

5. So he tied the lantern, which was made
of tin punched full of small holes, to the tail
of his kite. Then he pitched the kite, and,

after several attempts, succeeded in making it rise. Up it went, higher and higher, as Ray let out the string. When the string was all unwound, he tied it to a fence; and then he stood and gazed at his kite as it floated high up in the air.

6. While Ray was enjoying his sport, some people who were out on the street in the village, saw a strange light in the sky. They gathered in groups to watch it. Now it was still for a few seconds, then it seemed to be jumping up and down; then it made long sweeps back and forth through the air.

7. "What can it be?" said one person. "How strange!" said another. "It can not be a comet; for comets have tails," said a third. "Perhaps it's a big firefly," said another.

8. At last some of the men determined to find out what this strange light was— whether it was a hobgoblin dancing in the air, or something dropped from the sky. So off they started to get as near it as they could.

9. While this was taking place, Ray, who had got tired of standing, was seated in a fence corner, behind a tree. He could see

the men as they approached; but they did not see him.

10. When they were directly under the light, and saw what it was, they looked at each other, laughing, and said, "This is some boy's trick; and it has fooled us nicely. Let us keep the secret, and have our share of the joke."

11. Then they laughed again, and went back to the village; and some of the simple people there have not yet found out what that strange light was.

12. When the men had gone, Ray thought it was time for him to go; so he wound up his string, picked up his kite and lantern, and went home. His mother had been wondering what had become of him.

13. When she heard what he had been doing, she hardly knew whether to laugh or scold; but I think she laughed, and told him that it was time for him to go to bed.

DEFINITIONS.—2. Dāy′drēamṣ, *vain fancies.* Com păn′- ionṣ, *playmates, friends.* 5. At tĕmpts′, *trials, efforts.* 6. Groups, *several together, small assemblages.* Sweeps, *rapid movements in the line of a curve.* 7. Cŏm′et, *a brilliant heavenly body with a long, fiery tail.* 8. De tẽr′mĭned, *concluded, resolved.* Hŏb′gŏb lin, *an ugly fairy or imp.*

LESSON XLII.

BEWARE OF THE FIRST DRINK.

1. "Uncle Philip, as the day is fine, will you take a walk with us this morning?"

2. "Yes, boys. Let me get my hat and cane, and we will take a ramble. I will tell you a story as we go. Do you know poor old Tom Smith?"

3. "Know him! Why, Uncle Philip, every-body knows him. He is such a shocking drunkard, and swears so horribly."

4. "Well, I have known him ever since we were boys together. There was not a more decent, well-behaved boy among us. After he left school, his father died, and he was put into a store in the city. There, he fell into bad company.

5. "Instead of spending his evenings in reading, he would go to the theater and to balls. He soon learned to play cards, and of course to play for money. He lost more than he could pay.

6. "He wrote to his poor mother, and told her his losses. She sent him money to pay his debts, and told him to come home.

7. "He did come home. After all, he might still have been useful and happy, for his friends were willing to forgive the past. For a time, things went on well. He married a lovely woman, gave up his bad habits, and was doing well.

8. "But one thing, boys, ruined him forever. In the city, he had learned to take strong drink, and he said to me once, that when a man begins to drink, he never knows where it will end. 'Therefore,' said Tom, 'beware of the first drink!'

9. "It was not long before he began to follow his old habit. He knew the danger, but it seemed as if he could not resist his desire to drink. His poor mother soon died of grief and shame. His lovely wife followed her to the grave.

10. "He lost the respect of all, went on from bad to worse, and has long been a perfect sot. Last night, I had a letter from the city, stating that Tom Smith had been found guilty of stealing, and sent to the state prison for ten years.

11. "There I suppose he will die, for he is now old. It is dreadful to think to what an end he has come. I could not but think,

as I read the letter, of what he said to me years ago, 'Beware of the first drink!'

12. "Ah, my dear boys, when old Uncle Philip is gone, remember that he told you

the story of Tom Smith, and said to you, 'Beware of the first drink!' The man who does this will never be a drunkard."

DEFINITIONS.—3. Hŏr'ri bly, *in a dreadful manner, terribly.* 4. Dē'çent, *modest, respectable.* 9. Re ṣĭst', *withstand, overcome.* 10. Sŏt, *an habitual drunkard.* Guĭlt'y, *justly chargeable with a crime.*

3, 8.

LESSON XLIII.

SPEAK GENTLY.

1. Speak gently; it is better far
    To rule by love than fear:
    Speak gently; let no harsh words mar
    The good we might do here.

2. Speak gently to the little child;
    Its love be sure to gain;
    Teach it in accents soft and mild;
    It may not long remain.

3. Speak gently to the aged one;
    Grieve not the careworn heart:
    The sands of life are nearly run;
    Let such in peace depart.

4. Speak gently, kindly, to the poor;
    Let no harsh tone be heard;
    They have enough they must endure,
    Without an unkind word.

5. Speak gently to the erring; know
    They must have toiled in vain;
    Perhaps unkindness made them so;
    Oh, win them back again.

6. Speak gently: 't is a little thing
    Dropped in the heart's deep well;
    The good, the joy, which it may bring,
    Eternity shall tell.

George Washington Langford.

DEFINITIONS.—1. Mär, *injure, hurt.* 2. Ae′çents, *language, tones.* 4. En dūre′, *bear, suffer.* 5. Err′ing (ẽr′-), *sinning.* 6. E tẽr′ni ty, *the endless hereafter, the future.*

LESSON XLIV.

THE SEVEN STICKS.

1. A man had seven sons, who were always quarreling. They left their studies and work, to quarrel among themselves. Some bad men were looking forward to the death of their father, to cheat them out of their property by making them quarrel about it.

2. The good old man, one day, called his sons around him. He laid before them seven sticks, which were bound together. He said, "I will pay a hundred dollars to the one who can break this bundle."

3. Each one strained every nerve to break the bundle. After a long but vain trial, they all said that it could not be done.

4. "And yet, my boys," said the father, "nothing is easier to do." He then untied the bundle, and broke the sticks, one by one, with perfect ease.

5. "Ah!" said his sons, "it is easy enough to do it so; anybody could do it in that way."

6. Their father replied, "As it is with these sticks, so is it with you, my sons. So

long as you hold fast together and aid each other, you will prosper, and none can injure you.

7. "But if the bond of union be broken, it will happen to you just as it has to these sticks, which lie here broken on the ground."

> Home, city, country, all are prosperous found,
> When by the powerful link of union bound.

DEFINITIONS.—1. Chēat, *deceive, wrong.* Prŏp'er ty, *that which one owns—whether land, goods, or money.* 2. Bŭn'dle, *a number of things bound together.* 3. Nērve, *sinew, muscle.* 6. Prŏs'per, *succeed, do well.* 7. Un'ion (ūn'yun), *the state of being joined or united.*

LESSON XLV.

THE MOUNTAIN SISTER.

1. The home of little Jeannette is far away, high up among the mountains. Let us call her our mountain sister.

2. There are many things you would like to hear about her, but I can only tell you now how she goes with her father and brother, in the autumn, to help gather nuts for the long winter.

3. A little way down the mountain side is a chestnut wood.   Did you ever see a chest-nut tree?   In the spring its branches are covered with bunches of

creamy flow-ers, like long tassels.   All the hot sum-mer these are turning into sweet nuts, wrapped safely in large, prickly, green balls.

4. But when the frost of autumn comes, these prickly balls turn brown, and crack open.   Then you may see inside one, two, three, and even four, sweet, brown nuts.

5. When her father says, one night at supper time, "I think there will be a frost to-night," Jeannette knows very well what to do. She dances away early in the evening to her little bed, made in a box built up against the wall.

6. Soon she falls asleep to dream about

the chestnut wood, and the little brook that springs from rock to rock down under the tall, dark trees. She wakes with the first daylight, and is out of bed in a minute, when she hears her father's cheerful call, "Come, children; it is time to be off."

7. Their dinner is ready in a large basket. The donkey stands before the door with great bags for the nuts hanging at each side. They go merrily over the crisp, white frost to the chestnut trees. How the frost has opened the burs! It has done half their work for them already.

8. How they laugh and sing, and shout to each other as they fill their baskets! The sun looks down through the yellow leaves; the rocks give them mossy seats; the birds and squirrels wonder what these strange people are doing in their woods.

9. Jeannette really helps, though she is only a little girl; and her father says at night, that his Jane is a dear, good child. This makes her very happy. She thinks about it at night, when she says her prayers. Then she goes to sleep to dream of the merry autumn days.

10. Such is our little mountain sister, and

here is a picture of her far-away home. The
mountain life is ever a fresh and happy one.

DEFINITIONS.—3. Chĕst'nut (chĕs'nut), *a tree valuable for
its timber and its fruit.* Tăs'selṣ, *hanging ornaments, such as
are used on curtains.* Wrăpped (răpt), *completely covered up,
inclosed.* Prĭck'ly, *covered with sharp points.* 7. Crĭsp, *brit-
tle, sparkling.* Bûrṣ, *the rough coverings of seeds or nuts.*

LESSON XLVI.

HARRY AND THE GUIDEPOST.

1. The night was dark, the sun was hid
    Beneath the mountain gray,
And not a single star appeared
    To shoot a silver ray.

2. Across the heath the owlet flew,
    And screamed along the blast;
And onward, with a quickened step,
    Benighted Harry passed.

3. Now, in thickest darkness plunged,
    He groped his way to find;
And now, he thought he saw beyond,
    A form of horrid kind.

4. In deadly white it upward rose,
    Of cloak and mantle bare,
And held its naked arms across,
    To catch him by the hair.

5. Poor Harry felt his blood run cold,
    At what before him stood;
But then, thought he, no harm, I'm sure,
    Can happen to the good.

6. So, calling all his cour-
    age up,
He to the monster went;
And eager through the
    dismal gloom
His piercing eyes he bent.

7. And when he came well nigh the ghost
    That gave him such affright,
He clapped his hands upon his side,
    And loudly laughed outright.

8. For 't was a friendly guidepost stood,
    His wandering steps to guide;
And thus he found that to the good,
    No evil could betide.

9. Ah well, thought he, one thing I've learned,
    Nor shall I soon forget;
Whatever frightens me again,
    I'll march straight up to it.

10. And when I hear an idle tale,
    Of monster or of ghost,
I'll tell of this, my lonely walk,
    And one tall, white guidepost.

DEFINITIONS.—2. Hēath, *a place overgrown with shrubs.* Be nīght'ed, *overtaken by the night.* 3. Grōped, *felt his way in the dark.* Hŏr'rid, *hideous, frightful.* 6. Mŏn'ster, *a thing of unnatural size and shape.* Dĭṣ'mal, *dark, cheerless.* Piēr'çing, *sharp, penetrating.* 7. Ghōst (gōst), *a frightful object in white, an apparition.* 8. Guīde'pōst, *a post and sign set up at the forks of a road to direct travelers.* Be tīde', *befall, happen.* 10. I'dle, *of no account, foolish.*

LESSON XLVII.

THE MONEY AMY DIDN'T EARN.

1. Amy was a dear little girl, but she was too apt to waste time in getting ready to do her tasks, instead of doing them at once as she ought.

2. In the village in which she lived, **Mr.** Thornton kept a store where he sold fruit of all kinds, including berries in their season. One day he said to Amy, whose parents were quite poor, "Would you like to earn some money?"

3. "Oh, yes," replied she, "for I want some new shoes, and papa has no money to buy them with."

4. "Well, Amy," said Mr. Thornton, "I noticed some fine, ripe blackberries in Mr. Green's pasture to-day, and he said that any-body was welcome to them. I will pay you thirteen cents a quart for all you will pick for me."

5. Amy was delighted at the thought of earning some money; so she ran home to get a basket, intending to go immediately to pick the berries.

6. Then she thought she would like to know how much money she would get if she picked five quarts. With the help of her slate and pencil, she found out that she would get sixty-five cents.

7. "But supposing I should pick a dozen quarts," thought she, "how much should I earn then?" "Dear me," she said, after fig-

uring a while, "I should earn a dollar and
fifty-six cents."

8. Amy then found out what Mr. Thornton
would pay her for fifty, a hundred, and two
hundred quarts. It took her some time to

do this, and then it was so near dinner time
that she had to stay at home until afternoon.

9. As soon as dinner was over, she took

her basket and hurried to the pasture. Some boys had been there before dinner, and all the ripe berries were picked. She could not find enough to fill a quart measure.

10. As Amy went home, she thought of what her teacher had often told her—"Do your task at onee; then think about it," for "one doer is worth a hundred dreamers."

DEFINITIONS.—1. Tásks, *work which one has to do.* 2. Sēa'ṣon, *proper time of the year.* 4. Quạrt, *the fourth part of a gallon.* 7. Fĭg'ur ing, *computing, calculating.* 9. Hŭr'-ried, *went rapidly.* Mĕaṣ'ure, *vessel.*

LESSON XLVIII.

WHO MADE THE STARS?

1. "Mother, who made the stars, which light
   The beautiful blue sky?
   Who made the moon, so clear and bright,
   That rises up so high?"

2. "'Twas God, my child, the Glorious One,
   He formed them by his power;
   He made alike the brilliant sun,
   And every leaf and flower.

3. "He made your little feet to walk;
  Your sparkling eyes to see;
 Your busy, prattling tongue to talk,
  And limbs so light and free.

4 "He paints each fragrant flower that blows,
  With loveliness and bloom;
 He gives the violet and the rose
  Their beauty and perfume.

5. "Our various wants his hands supply;
  He guides us every hour;
 We're kept beneath his watchful eye,
  And guarded by his power.

6. "Then let your little heart, my love,
  Its grateful homage pay
 To that kind Friend, who, from above,
  Thus guides you every day.

7. "In all the changing scenes of time,
  On Him our hopes depend;
 In every age, in every clime,
  Our Father and our Friend."

DEFINITIONS.—2. Glō′ri oŭs, *excellent, exalted.* 3. Prăt′-tling, *talking lightly like a child.* 4. Blōwṣ, *blossoms.* Per-fūme′, *delightful odor.* 5. Vā′ri oŭs, *many and different.* 6. Hŏm′aġe, *respect.* 7. Sçēneṣ, *events.* Clīme, *climate, region.*

DEEDS OF KINDNESS.

1. One day, as two little boys were walking along the road, they overtook a woman carrying a large basket of apples.

2. The boys thought the woman looked very pale and tired; so they said, "Are you going to town? If you are, we will carry your basket."

3. "Thank you," replied the woman, "you are very kind: you see I am weak and ill." Then she told them that she was a widow, and had a lame son to support.

4. She lived in a cottage three miles away, and was now going to market to sell the apples which grew on the only tree in her little garden. She wanted the money to pay her rent.

5. "We are going the same way you are," said the boys. "Let us have the basket;" and they took hold of it, one on each side, and trudged along with merry hearts.

6. The poor widow looked glad, and said that she hoped their mother would not be angry with them. "Oh, no," they replied;

"our mother has taught us to be kind to everybody, and to be useful in any way that we can."

7. She then offered to give them a few of the ripest apples for their trouble.   "No,

thank you," said they; "we do not want any pay for what we have done."

8. When the widow got home, she told her lame son what had happened on the road,

and they were both made happier that day by the kindness of the two boys.

9. The other day, I saw a little girl stop and pick up a piece of orange peel, which she threw into the gutter. "I wish the boys would not throw orange peel on the sidewalk," said she. "Some one may tread upon it, and fall."

10. "That is right, my dear," I said. "It is a little thing for you to do what you have done, but it shows that you have a thoughtful mind and a feeling heart."

11. Perhaps some may say that these are *little* things. So they are; but we must not wait for occasions to do great things. We must begin with little labors of love.

DEFINITIONS.—3. Wĭd'ow, *a woman whose husband is dead.* 5. Trŭdġed, *walked.* 9. Gŭt'ter, *the lower ground or channel along the side of a road.* Trĕad, *step.* 11. Oe eā'ṣionṣ, *chances, opportunities.*

LESSON L.

THE ALARM CLOCK.

1. A lady, who found it not easy to wake in the morning as early as she wished,

bought an alarm clock. These clocks are so made as to strike with a loud whirring noise. at any hour the owner pleases to set them.

2. The lady placed her clock at the head of the bed, and at the right time she found herself roused by the long, rattling sound.

3. She arose at once, and felt better all day for her early rising. This lasted for some weeks. The alarm clock faithfully did its duty, and was plainly heard so long as it was obeyed.

4. But, after a time, the lady grew tired of early rising. When she was waked by the noise, she merely turned over in bed, and slept again.

5. In a few days, the clock ceased to rouse her from her sleep. It spoke just as loudly as ever; but she did not hear it, because she had been in the habit of not obeying it.

6. Finding that she might as well be without it, she resolved that when she heard the sound she would jump up.

7. Just so it is with conscience. If we will obey its voice, even in the most trifling things, we can always hear it, clear and strong.

8. But if we allow ourselves to do what we have some fears may not be quite right, we shall grow more and more sleepy, until the voice of conscience has no longer power to wake us.

DEFINITIONS.—1. A lärm', *a sudden sound calculated to awaken persons from sleep.* Whĭr'ring, *buzzing.* 2. Rouṣed, *waked.* Răt'tling, *giving quick, sharp noises in rapid succession.* 3. Fāith'ful ly, *in an exact and proper manner.* Dū'ty, *the right conduct or action.* 4. Mēre'ly, *simply.* 7. Cŏn'sciençe (kŏn'shens), *that within us which tells what is right and what is wrong, reason.* Trī'fling, *of little importance or value.* 8. Al low', *permit, suffer.*

LESSON LI.

SPRING.

1. The alder by the river
    Shakes out her powdery curls;
The willow buds in silver
    For little boys and girls.

2. The little birds fly over,
    And oh, how sweet they sing!
To tell the happy children
    That once again 't is Spring.

3. The gay green grass comes creeping
    So soft beneath their feet;
  The frogs begin to ripple
    A music clear and sweet.

4. And buttercups are coming,
    And scarlet columbine,
  And in the sunny meadows
    The dandelions shine.

5. And just as many daisies
    As their soft hands can hold,
  The little ones may gather,
    All fair in white and gold.

6. Here blows the warm red clover,
    There peeps the violet blue;
  Oh, happy little children!
    God made them all for you.

Celia Thaxter.

DEFINITIONS.—1. Al'der (al'-), *a tree which grows in moist land.* 3. Rip'ple, *to cause little waves of sound.*

LESSON LII.

TRUE COURAGE.

One cold winter's day, three boys were passing by a schoolhouse. The oldest was a bad boy, always in trouble himself, and trying to get others into trouble. The youngest, whose name was George, was a very good boy.

George wished to do right, but was very much wanting in courage. The other boys were named Henry and James. As they walked along, they talked as follows:

Henry. What fun it would be to throw a snowball against the schoolroom door, and make the teacher and scholars all jump!

James. *You* would jump, if you should. If the teacher did not catch you and whip you, he would tell your father, and you would get a whipping then; and that would make you jump higher than the scholars, I think.

Henry. Why, we would get so far off, before the teacher could come to the door, that he could not tell who we are. Here is a snowball just as hard as ice, and George would as soon throw it against the door as not.

James. Give it to him, and see. He would not dare to throw it.

Henry. Do you think George is a coward? You do not know him as well as I do.

Here, George, take this snowball, and show James that you are not such a coward as he thinks you are.

George. I am not afraid to throw it; but I do not want to. I do not see that it will do any good, or that there will be any fun in it.

James. There! I told you he would not dare to throw it.

Henry. Why, George, are you turning coward? I thought you did not fear anything. Come, save your credit, and throw it. I know you are not afraid.

George. Well, I am not afraid to throw. Give me the snowball. I would as soon throw it as not.

Whack! went the snowball against the door; and the boys took to their heels. Henry was laughing as heartily as he could, to think what a fool he had made of George.

George had a whipping for his folly, as he ought to have had. He was such a coward, that he was afraid of being called a coward. He did not dare refuse to do as Henry told him, for fear that he would be laughed at.

If he had been really a brave boy, he would have said, "Henry, do you suppose that I am so foolish as to throw that snowball, just because you want to have me? You may throw your own snowballs, if you please!"

Henry would, perhaps, have laughed at him, and called him a coward.

But George would have said, "Do you think that I care for your laughing? I do not think it right to throw the snowball. I will not do that which I think to be wrong, if the whole town should join with you in laughing."

This would have been real courage. Henry would have seen, at once, that it would do no good to laugh at a boy who had so bold a heart. You must have this fearless spirit, or you will get into trouble, and will be, and ought to be, disliked by all.

DEFINITIONS.—Sehŏl'arṣ, *children at school.* Whĭp'ping, *punishment.* Dâre, *have courage.* Crĕd'it, *reputation.* Heärt'i-ly, *freely, merrily.* Re fūṣe', *decline.* Fēar'less, *bold, brave.* Dis līked', *not loved.*

LESSON LIII.

THE OLD CLOCK.

1. In the old, old hall the old clock stands,
And round and round move the steady hands;
With its tick, tick, tick, both night and day,
While seconds and minutes pass away.

2. At the old, old clock oft wonders Nell,
   For she can't make out what it has to tell;

She has ne'er yet read, in prose or rhyme,
That it marks the silent course of time.

3. When I was a child, as Nell is now,
   And long ere Time had wrinkled my brow,
   The old, old clock both by night and by day,
   Said,—"Tick, tick, tick!" Time passes away.

DEFINITIONS.—2. Prōṣe, *the common language of men in talking or writing,* Rhȳme (rīme), *verse, poetry.* 3. Wrĭn'kled (rĭn'kld), *having creases or folds in the skin.* Brow, *the forehead.*

LESSON LIV.

THE WAVES.

1. "Where are we to go?" said the little waves to the great, deep sea.

"Go, my darlings, to the yellow sands: you will find work to do there."

2. "I want to play," said one little wave; "I want to see who can jump the highest."

"No; come on, come on," said an earnest wave; "mother must be right. I want to work."

3. "Oh, I dare not go," said another; "look at those great, black rocks close to the sands; I dare not go there, for they will tear me to pieces."

4. "Take my hand, sister," said the earnest wave; "let us go on together. How glorious it is to do some work."

5. "Shall we ever go back to mother?"

"Yes, when our work is done."

6. So one and all hurried on. Even the little wave that wanted to play, pressed on, and thought that work might be fun after all. The timid ones did not like to be left

behind, and they became earnest as they got nearer the sands.

7. After all, it was fun, pressing on one after another—jumping, laughing, running on to the broad, shining sands.

8. First, they came in their course to a great sand castle. Splash, splash! they all

went over it, and down it came. "Oh, what fun!" they cried.

9. "Mother told me to bring these sea-weeds; I will find a pretty place for them," said one—and she ran a long way over the sands, and left them among the pebbles. The pebbles cried, "We are glad you are come. We wanted washing."

10. "Mother sent these shells; I don't know where to put them," said a little fretful wave. "Lay them one by one on the sand, and do not break them," said the eldest wave.

11. And the little one went about its work, and learned to be quiet and gentle, for fear of breaking the shells.

12. "Where is my work?" said a great, full-grown wave. "This is mere play. The little ones can do this and laugh over it. Mother said there was work for *me*." And he came down upon some large rocks.

13. Over the rocks and into a pool he went, and he heard the fishes say, "The sea is coming. Thank you, great sea; you always send a big wave when a storm is nigh. Thank you, kind wave; we are all ready for you now."

14. Then the waves all went back over the wet sands, slowly and carelessly, for they were tired.

15. "All my shells are safe," said one.

16. And, "My seaweeds are left behind," said another.

17. "I washed all of the pebbles," said a third.

18. "And I—I only broke on a rock, and splashed into a pool," said the one that was so eager to work. "I have done no good, mother—no work at all."

19. "Hush!" said the sea. And they heard a child that was walking on the shore, say, "O mother, the sea has been here! Look, how nice and clean the sand is, and how clear the water is in that pool."

20. Then the sea said, "Hark!" and far away they heard the deep moaning of the coming storm

21. "Come, my darlings," said she; "you have done your work, now let the storm do its work."

DEFINITIONS.—6. Prĕssèd, *pushed, followed closely.* Tĭm'id, *wanting courage, not bold.* 10. Frĕt'fụl, *cross, peevish.* Eld'est, *first, foremost.* 20. Mōan'ing, *making a low, dull sound, muttering*

LESSON LV.

DON'T KILL THE BIRDS.

1. Don't kill the birds!
    the little birds,
    That sing about
    your door
Soon as the joyous
        Spring has come,
    And chilling storms are o'er.

2. The little birds! how sweet they sing!
    Oh, let them joyous live;
    And do not seek to take the life
    Which you can never give.

3. Don't kill the birds! the pretty birds,
    That play among the trees;

For earth would be a cheerless place,
    If it were not for these.

4. The little birds! how fond they play!
    Do not disturb their sport;
But let them warble forth their songs,
    Till winter cuts them short.

5. Do n't kill the birds! the happy birds,
    That bless the field and grove;
So innocent to look upon,
    They claim our warmest love.

6. The happy birds, the tuneful birds,
    How pleasant 't is to see!
No spot can be a cheerless place
    Where'er their presence be.

DEFINITIONS.—4. Dis tûrb′, *interfere with.* Wạr′ble, *to trill, to carol.* 5. In′no çent, *pure, harmless.* 6. Tūne′fụl, *musical, melodious.* Prĕṣ′ençe, *state of being at hand, existence.*

LESSON LVI.

WHEN TO SAY NO.

1. Though "No" is a very little word, it is not always easy to say it; and the not doing so, often causes trouble.

2. When we are asked to stay away from school, and spend in idleness or mischief the time which ought to be spent in study, we should at once say "No."

3. When we are urged to loiter on our way to school, and thus be late, and interrupt our teacher and the school, we should say "No." When some schoolmate wishes us to whisper or play in the schoolroom, we should say "No."

4. When we are tempted to use angry or wicked words, we should remember that the eye of God is always upon us, and should say "No."

5. When we have done anything wrong, and are tempted to conceal it by falsehood, we should say "No, we can not tell a lie; it is wicked and cowardly."

6. If we are asked to do anything which we know to be wrong, we should not fear to say "No."

7. If we thus learn to say "No," we shall avoid much trouble, and be always safe.

DEFINITIONS.—1. Caus′es, *makes.* 2. I′dle ness, *a doing nothing, laziness.* 3. Urġed, *asked repeatedly.* Loi′ter, *linger, delay.* In ter rŭpt′, *disturb, hinder.* 4. Tĕmpt′ed, *led by evil circumstances.* 5. Con çēal′, *hide.* False′hōŏd, *untruth.*

3, 10.

LESSON LVII.

WHICH LOVED BEST?

"I love you, mother," said little John;
Then, forgetting work, his cap went on,
And he was off to the garden swing,
Leaving his mother the wood to bring.

2. "I love you, mother," said rosy Nell;
   "I love you better than tongue can tell;"

Then she teased and pouted full half the day,
Till her mother rejoiced when she went to play.

3. "I love you, mother," said little Fan;
"To-day I'll help you all I can;
How glad I am that school does n't keep!"
So she rocked the baby till it fell asleep.

4. Then, stepping softly, she took the broom,
And swept the floor, and dusted the room;
Busy and happy all day was she,
Helpful and cheerful as child could be.

5. "I love you, mother," again they said—
Three little children going to bed;
How do you think that mother guessed
Which of them really loved her best?

Joy Allison.

LESSON LVIII.

JOHN CARPENTER.

1. John Carpenter did not like to buy toys that somebody else had made. He liked the fun of making them himself. The thought that they were his own work delighted him.

2. Tom Austin, one of his playmates, thought a toy was worth nothing unless it cost a great deal of money. He never tried to make anything, but bought all his toys.

3. "Come and look at my horse," said he, one day. "It cost a dollar, and it is such a beauty! Come and see it."

4. John was soon admiring his friend's

horse; and he was examining it carefully, to see how it was made. The same evening he began to make one for himself.

5. He went into the wood shed, and picked

out two pieces of wood—one for the head of his horse, the other for the body. It took him two or three days to shape them to his satisfaction.

6. His father gave him a bit of red leather for a bridle, and a few brass nails, and his mother found a bit of old fur with which he made a mane and tail for his horse.

7. But what about the wheels? This puzzled him. At last he thought he would go to a turner's shop, and see if he could not get some round pieces of wood which might suit his purpose.

8. He found a large number of such pieces among the shavings on the floor, and asked permission to take a few of them. The turner asked him what he wanted them for, and he told him about his horse.

9. "Oh," said the man, laughing, "if you wish it, I will make some wheels for your horse. But mind, when it is finished, you must let me see it."

10. John promised to do so, and he soon ran home with the wheels in his pocket. The next evening, he went to the turner's shop with his horse all complete, and was told that he was an ingenious little fellow.

11. Proud of this compliment, he ran to his friend Tom, crying, "Now then, Tom, here is my horse,—look!"

12. "Well, that is a funny horse," said Tom; "where did you buy it?" "I did n't buy it," replied John; I made it."

13. "You made it yourself! Oh, well, it 's a good horse for you to make. But it is not so good as mine. Mine cost a dollar, and yours did n't cost anything."

14. "It was real fun to make it, though," said John, and away he ran with his horse rolling after him.

15. Do you want to know what became of John? Well, I will tell you. He studied hard in school, and was called the best scholar in his class. When he left school, he went to work in a machine shop. He is now a master workman, and will soon have a shop of his own.

DEFINITIONS.—4. Ad mīr'ing, *looking at with pleasure.* Ex ăm'in ing, *looking at every point.* 6. Lĕath'er, *the skin of an animal prepared for use.* 7. Pŭz'zled, *perplexed, caused trouble.* Tûrn'er, *one who shapes wooden or metal articles by means of a lathe.* 8. Shāv'ings, *the thin ribbons of wood which a carpenter makes in planing.* Per mĭs'sion, *privilege, consent.* 10. Com plēte', *finished.* In ġēn'ioŭs, *skillful.* 11. Cŏm'pliment, *praise, approbation.*

LESSON LIX.

PERSEVERE.

1. The fisher who draws in his net too soon,
   Won't have any fish to sell;
   The child who shuts up his book too soon,
   Won't learn any lessons well.

2 If you would have your learning stay,
   Be patient,—do n't learn too fast:
   The man who travels a mile each day,
   May get round the world at last.

LESSON LX.

THE CONTENTED BOY.

Mr. Lenox was one morning riding by himself. He got off from his horse to look at something on the roadside. The horse broke away from him, and ran off. Mr. Lenox ran after him, but soon found that he could not catch him.

A little boy at work in a field near the road, heard the horse. As soon as he saw him running from his master, the boy ran very quickly to the middle of the road, and, catching the horse by the bridle, stopped him till Mr. Lenox came up.

Mr. Lenox. Thank you, my good boy, you have caught my horse very nicely. What shall I give you for your trouble?

Boy. I want nothing, sir.

Mr. L. You want nothing? So much the better for you. Few men can say as much. But what were you doing in the field?

B. I was rooting up weeds, and tending the sheep that were feeding on turnips.

Mr. L. Do you like to work?

B. Yes, sir, very well, this fine weather.

Mr. L. But would you not rather play?

B. This is not hard work. It is almost as good as play.

Mr. L. Who set you to work?

B. My father, sir.

Mr. L. What is your name?

B. Peter Hurdle, sir.

Mr. L. How old are you?

B. Eight years old, next June.

Mr. L. How long have you been here?

B. Ever since six o'clock this morning.

Mr. L. Are you not hungry?

B. Yes, sir, but I shall go to dinner soon.

Mr. L. If you had a dime now, what would you do with it?

B. I do n't know, sir. I never had so much.

Mr. L. Have you no playthings?

B. Playthings? What are they?

Mr. L. Such things as ninepins, marbles, tops, and wooden horses.

B. No, sir. Tom and I play at football in winter, and I have a jumping rope. I had a hoop, but it is broken.

Mr. L. Do you want nothing else?

B. I have hardly time to play with what I have. I have to drive the cows, and to run on errands, and to ride the horses to the fields, and that is as good as play.

Mr. L. You could get apples and cakes, if you had money, you know.

B. I can have apples at home. As for cake, I do not want that. My mother makes me a pie now and then, which is as good.

Mr. L. Would you not like a knife to cut sticks?

B. I have one. Here it is. Brother Tom gave it to me.

Mr. L. Your shoes are full of holes. Don't you want a new pair?

B. I have a better pair for Sundays.

Mr. L. But these let in water.

B. I do not mind that, sir.

Mr. L. Your hat is all torn, too.

B. I have a better one at home.

Mr. L. What do you do when it rains?

B. If it rains very hard when I am in the field, I get under a tree for shelter.

Mr. L. What do you do, if you are hungry before it is time to go home?

B. I sometimes eat a raw turnip.

Mr. L. But if there is none?

B. Then I do as well as I can without. I work on, and never think of it.

Mr. L. Why, my little fellow, I am glad to see that you are so contented. Were you ever at school?

B. No, sir. But father means to send me next winter.

Mr. L. You will want books then.

B. Yes, sir; each boy has a Spelling Book, a Reader, and a Testament.

Mr. L. Then I will give them to you. Tell your father so, and that it is because you are an obliging, contented little boy.

B. I will, sir. Thank you.

Mr. L. Good by, Peter.

B. Good morning, sir.

Dr. John Aiken.

DEFINITIONS.—Rōōt′ing, *pulling up by the roots.* Tĕnd′ing, *watching, attending.* Tûr′nip, *a vegetable.* Wĕath′er, *state of the atmosphere.* Er′rands̤, *messages.* Ra̤w, *not cooked.* Tĕs′tament, *the last twenty-seven books of the Bible.*

LESSON LXI.

LITTLE GUSTAVA.

1. Little Gustava sits in the sun,
   Safe in the porch, and the little drops run
   From the icicles under the eaves so fast,
   For the bright spring sun shines warm at last,
       And glad is little Gustava.

2. She wears a quaint little scarlet cap,
   And a little green bowl she holds in her lap,
   Filled with bread and milk to the brim,
   And a wreath of marigolds round the rim:
       "Ha! ha!" laughs little Gustava.

3. Up comes her little gray, coaxing cat,
   With her little pink nose, and she mews, "What's
       that?"
   Gustava feeds her,—she begs for more,
   And a little brown hen walks in at the door:
       "Good day!" cries little Gustava.

4. She scatters crumbs for the little brown hen,
   There comes a rush and a flutter, and then
   Down fly her little white doves so sweet,
   With their snowy wings and their crimson feet:
       "Welcome!" cries little Gustava.

5. So dainty and eager they pick up the crumbs.
   But who is this through the doorway comes?

Little Scotch terrier, little dog Rags,
Looks in her face, and his funny tail wags:
"Ha! ha!" laughs little Gustava.

6. "You want some breakfast, too?" and down
She sets her bowl on the brick floor brown,
And little dog Rags drinks up her milk,
While she strokes his shaggy locks, like silk:
"Dear Rags!" says little Gustava.

7. Waiting without stood sparrow and crow,
Cooling their feet in the melting snow.

" Won't you come in, good folk?" she cried,
.But they were too bashful, and staid outside,
 Though " Pray come in!" cried Gustava.

8. So the last she threw them, and knelt on the mat,
 With doves, and biddy, and dog, and cat.
 And her mother came to the open house door:
 " Dear little daughter, I bring you some more,
 My merry little Gustava."

9. Kitty and terrier, biddy and doves,
 All things harmless Gustava loves,
 The shy, kind creatures 't is joy to feed,
 And, oh! her breakfast is sweet indeed
 To happy little Gustava!

Celia Thaxter.

DEFINITIONS.—1. Gus tä′vȧ, *a girl's name.* I′çi eleş, *water frozen in lonɡ. needle-like shapes.* Eaveş (ēvz), *the lower edges of a roof.* 2. Quäint, *odd.* Măr′i ḡōld, *a yellow flower.* 8. Knĕlt, *bent on her knees.* Bĭd′dy, *chicken.*

LESSON LXII.

THE INSOLENT BOY.

1. James Selton was one of the most inso-lent boys in the village where he lived. He would rarely pass people in the street with-out being guilty of some sort of abuse.

2. If a person were well dressed he would cry out, " Dandy! " If a person's clothes were dirty or torn, he would throw stones at him, and annoy him in every way.

3. One afternoon, just as the school was dismissed, a stranger passed through the village. His dress was plain and somewhat old, but neat and clean. He carried a cane in his hand, on the end of which was a bundle, and he wore a broad-brimmed hat.

4. No sooner did James see the stranger, than he winked to his playmates, and said, "Now for some fun!" He then silently went toward the stranger from behind, and, knocking off his hat, ran away.

5. The man turned and saw him, but James was out of hearing before he could speak. The stranger put on his hat, and went on his way. Again did James approach; but this time, the man caught him by the arm, and held him fast.

6. However, he contented himself with looking James a moment in the face, and then pushed him from him. No sooner did the naughty boy find himself free again, than he began to pelt the stranger with dirt and stones.

7. But he was much frightened when the "rowdy," as he foolishly called the man, was struck on the head by a brick, and badly hurt. All the boys now ran away, and James skulked across the fields to his home.

8. As he drew near the house, his sister Caroline came out to meet him, holding up

a beautiful gold chain and some new books for him to see.

9. She told James, as fast as she could talk, that their uncle, who had been away several years, had come home, and was now in the house; that he had brought beautiful presents for the whole family; that he had left his carriage at the tavern, a mile or two off, and walked on foot, so as to surprise his brother, their father.

10. She said, that while he was coming through the village, some wicked boys threw stones at him, and hit him just over the eye, and that mother had bound up the wound. "But what makes you look so pale?" asked Caroline, changing her tone.

11. The guilty boy told her that nothing was the matter with him; and running into the house, he went upstairs into his chamber. Soon after, he heard his father calling him to come down. Trembling from head to foot, he obeyed. When he reached the parlor door, he stood, fearing to enter.

12. His mother said, "James, why do you not come in? You are not usually so bashful. See this beautiful watch, which your uncle has brought for you."

3, 11.

13. What a sense of shame did James now feel! Little Caroline seized his arm, and pulled him into the room. But he hung down his head, and covered his face with his hands.

14. His uncle went up to him, and kindly taking away his hands, said, "James, will you not bid me welcome?" But quickly starting back, he cried, "Brother, this is not your son. It is the boy who so shamefully insulted me in the street!"

15. With surprise and grief did the good father and mother learn this. His uncle was ready to forgive him, and forget the injury. But his father would never permit James to have the gold watch, nor the beautiful books, which his uncle had brought for him.

16. The rest of the children were loaded with presents. James was obliged to content himself with seeing them happy. He never forgot this lesson so long as he lived. It cured him entirely of his low and insolent manners.

DEFINITIONS.—1. In'so lent, *rude, insulting.* Râre'ly, *hardly ever.* A būse', *ill usage.* 2. Dăn'dy, *a fop.* 3. Dismĭssed', *let out.* 6. Năugh'ty (nạ'ty), *bad, wicked.* 7.

Row'dy, *a low fellow, who engages in fights.*   Skŭlked, *went in a sneaking manner.*   9. Un'cle, *the brother of one's father or mother.*   Tăv'ern, *a small hotel.*   14. Shāme'fụl ly, *disgracefully.*   In sŭlt'ed, *treated with abuse.*   15. In'ju ry, *harm done.* 16. En tīre'ly, *altogether.*

LESSON LXIII.

WE ARE SEVEN.

1. I met a little cottage girl:
      She was eight years old, she said;
   Her hair was thick with many a curl,
      That clustered round her head.

2. She had a rustic, woodland air,
      And she was wildly clad:
   Her eyes were fair, and very fair;—
      Her beauty made me glad.

3. "Sisters and brothers, little maid,
      How many may you be?"
   "How many? Seven in all," she said,
      And, wondering, looked at me.

4. "And where are they? I pray you tell."
      She answered, "Seven are we;
   And two of us at Conway dwell,
      And two are gone to sea.

5. "Two of us in the churchyard lie,
   My sister and my brother;
And, in the churchyard cottage, I
   Dwell near them with my mother."

6. "You say that two at Conway dwell,
   And two are gone to sea,
Yet ye are seven! I pray you tell,
   Sweet maid, how this may be."

7. Then did the little maid reply,
   "Seven boys and girls are we;
   Two of us in the churchyard lie,
   Beneath the churchyard tree."

8. "You run about, my little maid,
   Your limbs, they are alive;
   If two are in the churchyard laid,
   Then ye are only five."

9. "Their graves are green, they may be seen,"
   The little maid replied,
   "Twelve steps or more from mother's door,
   And they are side by side.

10. "My stockings there I often knit,
    My kerchief there I hem;
    And there upon the ground I sit,
    And sing a song to them.

11. "And often after sunset, sir,
    When it is light and fair,
    I take my little porringer,
    And eat my supper there.

12. "The first that died was sister Jane;
    In bed she moaning lay,

Till God released her from her pain;
 And then she went away.

13. "So in the churchyard she was laid;
 And, when the grass was dry,
Together round her grave we played,
 My brother John and I.

14. "And when the ground was white with snow,
 And I could run and slide,
My brother John was forced to go,
 And he lies by her side."

15. "How many are you, then?" said I,
 "If they two are in heaven?"
Quick was the little maid's reply,
 "O master! we are seven."

16. "But they are dead; those two are dead!
 Their spirits are in heaven!"
'Twas throwing words away: for still
The little maid would have her will,
 And said, "Nay, we are seven."

William Wordsworth.

DEFINITIONS.—1. Clŭs′tered, *hung in bunches.* 2. Rŭs′tie, *country-like.* 10. Kẽr′chĭef, *handkerchief.* 11. Pŏr′rĭn ġer, *a small dish for soup or porridge.* 12. Re lēased′, *freed, relieved.*

LESSON LXIV.

MARY'S DIME.

1. There! I have drawn the chairs into the right corners, and dusted the room nicely. How cold papa and mamma will be when they return from their long ride! It is not time to toast the bread yet, and I am tired of reading.

2. What shall I do? Somehow, I can't help thinking about the pale face of that little beggar girl all the time. I can see the glad light filling her eyes, just as plain as I did when I laid the dime in her little dirty hand.

3. How much I had thought of that dime, too! Grandpa gave it to me a whole month ago, and I had kept it ever since in my red box upstairs; but those sugar apples looked so beautiful, and were so cheap—only a dime apiece—that I made up my mind to have one.

4. I can see her—the beggar girl, I mean—as she stood there in front of the store, in her old hood and faded dress, looking at the candies laid all in a row. I wonder

what made me say, "Little girl, what do you
want?"

5. How she stared at me, just as if nobody
had spoken kindly to her before. I guess

she thought I was sorry for her, for she said,
so earnestly and sorrowfully, "I was thinking how good one of those gingerbread rolls
would taste. I have n't had anything to eat
to-day."

6. Now, I thought to myself, "Mary Williams, you have had a good breakfast and a good dinner this day, and this poor girl has not had a mouthful. You can give her your dime; she needs it a great deal more than you do."

7. I could not resist that little girl's sorrowful, hungry look—so I dropped the dime right into her hand, and, without waiting for her to speak, walked straight away. I'm so glad I gave her the dime, if I did have to go without the apple lying there in the window, and looking just like a real one.

DEFINITIONS.—1. Tōast, *to scorch until brown by the heat of a fire.* 3. Chēap, *low in price.* A piēçe', *each.* 4. Hŏŏd, *a soft covering for the head.* Fād'ed, *having lost freshness of color.* 5. Stâred, *looked earnestly.* Sŏr'row fụl ly, *full of sadness.* Gĭn'ger brĕad, *a kind of sweet cake flavored with ginger.*

LESSON LXV.

MARY DOW.

1. "Come in, little stranger," I said,
    As she tapped at my half-open door;
  While the blanket, pinned over her head,
  Just reached to the basket she bore.

2. A look full of innocence fell
    From her modest and pretty blue eye,
As she said, "I have matches to sell,
    And hope you are willing to buy.

3. "A penny a bunch is the price,
    I think you'll not find it too much;
They are tied up so even and nice,
    And ready to light with a touch."

4. I asked, "What's your name, little girl?"
    "'T is Mary," said she, "Mary Dow;"

And carelessly tossed off a curl,
That played on her delicate brow.

5. "My father was lost on the deep;
The ship never got to the shore;
And mother is sad, and will weep,
To hear the wind blow and sea roar.

6. "She sits there at home, without food,
Beside our poor, sick Willy's bed;
She paid all her money for wood,
And so I sell matches for bread.

7. "I'd go to the yard and get chips,
But then it would make me too sad
To see the men building the ships,
And think they had made one so bad.

8. "But God, I am sure, who can take
Such fatherly care of a bird,
Will never forget nor forsake
The children who trust in his word.

9. "And now, if I only can sell
The matches I brought out to-day,
I think I shall do very well,
And we shall rejoice at the pay."

10. "Fly home, little bird," then I thought,
    "Fly home, full of joy, to your nest;"
For I took all the matches she brought,
    And Mary may tell you the rest.

DEFINITIONS.—1. Blăn'ket, *a square of loosely woven woolen cloth.* 2. Mătch'eş, *small splints of wood, one end of which has been dipped in a preparation which will take fire by rubbing.* 3. Pĕn'ny, *cent.* 4. Dĕl'i eate, *soft and fair.* 8. For sāke', *leave, reject.*

LESSON LXVI.

THE LITTLE LOAF.

1. Once when there was a famine, a rich baker sent for twenty of the poorest children in the town, and said to them, "In this basket there is a loaf for each of you. Take it, and come back to me every day at this hour till God sends us better times."

2. The hungry children gathered eagerly about the basket, and quarreled for the bread, because each wished to have the largest loaf. At last they went away without even thanking the good gentleman.

3. But Gretchen, a poorly-dressed little girl, did not quarrel or struggle with the rest,

but remained standing modestly in the distance. When the ill-behaved girls had left, she took the smallest loaf, which alone was left in the basket, kissed the gentleman's hand, and went home.

4. The next day the children were as ill-behaved as before, and poor, timid Gretchen received a loaf scarcely half the size of the one she got the first day. When she came home, and her mother cut the loaf open, many new, shining pieces of silver fell out of it.

5. Her mother was very much alarmed, and said, "Take the money back to the good gentleman at once, for it must have got into the dough by accident. Be quick, Gretchen! be quick!"

6. But when the little girl gave the rich man her mother's message, he said, "No, no, my child, it was no mistake. I had the silver pieces put into the smallest loaf to reward you. Always be as contented, peaceable, and grateful as you now are. Go home now, and tell your mother that the money is your own."

DEFINITIONS.—1. Făm'ĭne, *a general scarcity of food.* Lōaf, *a molded mass of regular shape* (as of bread or cake). 3. Grĕtch'en, *a girl's name—the shortened form, or pet name, for Marguerite.* Re māined', *staid.* Dĭs'tançe, *place which is far off.* Ill-be hāved', *rude, having bad manners.* 5. Aç'çi-dent, *mistake.* 6. Mĕs'saġe, *word sent, communication.* Pēaçe'-a ble, *quiet, gentle.*

LESSON LXVII.

SUSIE AND ROVER.

1. "Mamma," said Susie Dean, one summer's morning, "may I go to the woods, and pick berries?"

2. "Yes," replied Mrs. Dean, "but you must take Rover with you."

3. Susie brought her little basket, and her mother put up a nice lunch for her. She tied down the cover, and fastened a tin cup to it.

4. The little girl called Rover—a great Newfoundland dog—and gave him a tin pail to carry. "If I bring it home full, mamma," she said, "won't you make some berry cakes for tea?"

5. Away she tripped, singing as she went down the lane and across the pasture. When she got to the woods, she put her dinner basket down beside a tree, and began to pick berries.

6. Rover ran about, chasing a squirrel or a rabbit now and then, but never straying far from Susie.

7. The tin pail was not a very small one. By the time it was two thirds full, Susie began to feel hungry, and thought she would eat her lunch.

8. Rover came and took his place at her side as soon as she began to eat. Did she not give him some of the lunch? No, she was in a selfish mood, and did no such thing.

9. "There, Rover, run away! there's a good dog," she said; but Rover staid near her, watching her steadily with his clear brown eyes.

10. The meat he wanted so much, was soon eaten up; and all he got of the nice dinner, was a small crust of gingerbread that Susie threw away.

11. After dinner, Susie played a while by

the brook. She threw sticks into the water, and Rover swam in and brought them back. Then she began to pick berries again.

12. She did not enjoy the afternoon as she did the morning. The sunshine was as bright, the berries were as sweet and plentiful, and she was neither tired nor hungry.

13. But good, faithful Rover was hungry, and she had not given him even one piece of meat. She tried to forget how selfish she had been; but she could not do so, and quite early she started for home.

14. When she was nearly out of the woods, a rustling in the underbrush attracted her attention. "I wonder if that is a bird or a squirrel," said she to herself. "If I can catch it, how glad I shall be!"

15. She tried to make her way quietly through the underbrush; but what was her terror when she saw a large snake coiled up before her, prepared for a spring!

16. She was so much frightened that she could not move; but brave Rover saw the snake, and, springing forward, seized it by the neck and killed it.

17. When the faithful dog came and rubbed his head against her hand, Susie put her

3, 12.

arms around his neck, and burst into tears. "O Rover," she cried, "you dear, good dog! How sorry I am that I was so selfish!"

18. Rover understood the tone of her voice, if he did not understand her words, and capered about in great glee, barking all the time. You may be sure that he had a plentiful supper that evening.

19. Susie never forgot the lesson of that day. She soon learned to be on her guard against a selfish spirit, and became a happier and more lovable little girl.

Mrs. M. O. Johnson—Adapted.

DEFINITIONS.—8. Sĕlf'ish, *thinking and caring only for one's self.* Mōōd, *state of mind.* 9. Stĕad'i ly, *constantly.* 12. Plĕn'ti fṳl, *abundant.* Nēi'ther, *not the one or the other.* 14. Un'der brŭsh, *shrubs or small bushes in a forest.* At-trăet'ed, *drew.* At tĕn'tion, *earnest thought.* 15. Tĕr'ror, *fright, fear.* 18. Cā'pered, *frisked.*

LESSON LXVIII.

THE VIOLET.

1. Down in a green and shady bed,
    A modest violet grew;
Its stalk was bent, it hung its head,
    As if to hide from view.

CUIPON

2. And yet it was a lovely flower,
   Its colors bright and fair;
   It might have graced a rosy bower
   Instead of hiding there.

3. Yet there it was content to bloom,
   In modest tints arrayed,
   And there it spread its sweet perfume,
   Within the silent shade.

4. Then let me to the valley go,
   This pretty flower to see;
   That I may also learn to grow
   In sweet humility.

Jane Taylor.

LESSON LXIX.

NO CROWN FOR ME.

1. "Will you come with us, Susan?" cried several little girls to a schoolmate. "We are going to the woods; do come, too."

2. "I should like to go with you very much," replied Susan, with a sigh; "but I can not finish the task grandmother set me to do."

3. "How tiresome it must be to stay at home to work on a holiday!" said one of the girls, with a toss of her head. "Susan's grandmother is too strict."

4. Susan heard this remark, and, as she bent her head over her task, she wiped away a tear, and thought of the pleasant afternoon the girls would spend gathering wild flowers in the woods.

5. Soon she said to herself, "What harm can there be in moving the mark grandmother put in the stocking? The woods must be very beautiful to-day, and how I should like to be in them!"

6. "Grandmother," said she, a few minutes afterwards, "I am ready, now." "What, so

soon, Susan?" Her grandmother took the work, and looked at it very closely.

7. "True, Susan," said she, laying great stress on each word; "true, I count twenty turns from the mark; and, as you have never deceived me, you may go and amuse yourself as you like the rest of the day."

8. Susan's cheeks were scarlet, and she did not say, "Thank you." As she left the cottage, she walked slowly away, not singing as usual.

9. "Why, here is Susan!" the girls cried, when she joined their company; "but what is the matter? Why have you left your dear, old grandmother?" they tauntingly added.

10. "There is nothing the matter." As Susan repeated these words, she felt that she was trying to deceive herself. She had acted a lie. At the same time she remembered her grandmother's words, "You have never deceived me."

11. "Yes, I have deceived her," said she to herself. "If she knew all, she would never trust me again."

12. When the little party had reached an open space in the woods, her companions ran about enjoying themselves; but Susan sat on

the grass, wishing she were at home confessing her fault.

13. After a while Rose cried out, "Let us make a crown of violets, and put it on the head of the best girl here."

14. "It will be easy enough to make the crown, but not so easy to decide who is to wear it," said Julia.

15. "Why, Susan is to wear it, of course," said Rose: "is she not said to be the best girl in school, and the most obedient at home?"

16. "Yes, yes; the crown shall be for Su-

san," cried the other girls, and they began to make the crown. It was soon finished.

17. "Now, Susan," said Rose, "put it on in a very dignified way, for you are to be our queen."

18. As these words were spoken, the crown was placed on her head. In a moment she snatched it off, and threw it on the ground, saying, "No crown for me; I do not deserve it."

19. The girls looked at her with surprise. "I have deceived my grandmother," said she, while tears flowed down her cheeks. "I altered the mark she put in the stocking, that I might join you in the woods."

20. "Do you call that wicked?" asked one of the girls.

"I am quite sure it is; and I have been miserable all the time I have been here."

21. Susan now ran home, and as soon as she got there she said, with a beating heart, "O grandmother! I deserve to be punished, for I altered the mark you put in the stocking. Do forgive me; I am very sorry and unhappy."

22. "Susan," said her grandmother, "I knew it all the time; but I let you go out, hoping

that your own conscience would **tell** you of your sin. I am so glad that you have confessed your fault and your sorrow."

23. "When shall I be your own little girl again?" "Now," was the quick reply, and Susan's grandmother kissed her forehead.

DEFINITIONS.—3. Tïre'sŏme, *tedious, wearisome.* 7. Strĕss, *force, emphasis.* 9. Cŏm'pa ny, *a number of persons together.* Täunt'ing ly, *in a disagreeable, reproachful manner.* 12. Con-fĕss'ing, *telling of, acknowledging.* Fạult, *wrongdoing, sin.* 17. Dĭḡ'ni fïed, *respectful, stately.* 19. Al'tered (ạl'-), *changed.* 20. Mĭṣ'er a ble, *wretched, very unhappy.* 23. Fŏre'head (fŏr'ed), *the front part of the head above the eyes.*

LESSON LXX.

YOUNG SOLDIERS.

1. Oh, were you ne'er a schoolboy,
   And did you never train,
And feel that swelling of the heart
   You ne'er can feel again?

2. Did you never meet, far down the street,
   With plumes and banners gay,
While the kettle, for the kettledrum,
   Played your march, march away?

3. It seems to me but yesterday,
　　Nor scarce so long ago,
　Since all our school their muskets took,
　　To charge the fearful foe.

4. Our muskets were of cedar wood,
　　With ramrods bright and new;
　With bayonets forever set,
　　And painted barrels, too.

5. We charged upon a flock of geese,
　　And put them all to flight—
　Except one sturdy gander
　　That thought to show us fight.

6. But, ah! we knew a thing or two;
   Our captain wheeled the van;
   We routed him, we scouted him,
   Nor lost a single man!

7. Our captain was as brave a lad
   As e'er commission bore;
   And brightly shone his new tin sword;
   A paper cap he wore.

8. He led us up the steep hillside,
   Against the western wind,
   While the cockerel plume that decked his
   head
   Streamed bravely out behind.

9. We shouldered arms, we carried arms,
   We charged the bayonet;
   And woe unto the mullein stalk
   That in our course we met!

10. At two o'clock the roll we called,
    And till the close of day,
With fearless hearts, though tired limbs,
    We fought the mimic fray,—
Till the supper bell, from out the dell,
    Bade us march, march away.

DEFINITIONS.—2. Kĕt'tle drŭm, *a drum made of a copper vessel shaped like a kettle.* 3. Mŭs'ket, *a kind of gun.* 4. Cē'dar, *a very durable kind of wood.* Bāy'o net, *a sharp piece of steel on the end of a gun.* Băr'rel, *the long metal tube forming part of a gun.* 5. Stûr'dy, *stubborn, bold.* 6. Văn, *the front.* Rout'ed, *put to flight.* Scout'ed, *made fun of.* 7. Com mĭs'sion, *a writing to show power.* 8. Cŏck'er el, *a young chicken-cock.* 9. Chärġed, *made an onset.* Mŭl'lein, *a tall plant that grows in neglected fields.* 10. Frāy, *fight, contest.*

LESSON LXXI.

HOW WILLIE GOT OUT OF THE SHAFT.

1. Willie's aunt sent him for a birthday present a little writing book. There was a place in the book for a pencil. Willie thought a great deal of this little book, and always kept it in his pocket.

2. One day, his mother was very busy, and he called his dog, and said, "Come, Caper, let us have a play."

3. When Willie's mother missed him, she went to the door and looked out, and could not see him anywhere; but she knew that Caper was with him, and thought they would come back before long.

4. She waited an hour, and still they did not come. When she came to the gate by the road, she met Mr. Lee, and told him how long Willie had been gone. Mr. Lee thought he must have gone to sleep under the trees. So they went to all the trees under which Willie was in the habit of playing, but he was nowhere to be found.

5. By this time the sun had gone down. The news that Willie was lost soon spread over the neighborhood, and all the men and women turned out to hunt. They hunted all night.

6. The next morning the neighbors were gathered round, and all were trying to think what to do next, when Caper came bounding into the room. There was a string tied round his neck, and a bit of paper tied to it.

7. Willie's father, Mr. Lee, took the paper, and saw that it was a letter from Willie. He read it aloud. It said, "O father! come to me. I am in the big hole in the pasture."

8. Everybody ran at once to the far corner of the pasture; and there was Willie, alive and well, in the shaft. Oh, how glad he was when his father caught him in his arms, and lifted him out!

9. Now I will tell you how Willie came to be in the shaft. He and Caper went to the pasture field, and came to the edge of the shaft and sat down. In bending over

to see how deep it was, he lost his balance, and fell in. He tried very hard to get out, but could not.

10. When the good little dog saw that his master was in the shaft, he would not leave him, but ran round and round, reaching down and trying to pull him out. But while Caper was pulling Willie by the coat sleeves, a piece of sod gave way under his feet, and he fell in too.

11. Willie called for his father and mother as loud as he could call; but he was so far away from the house that no one could hear him.

12. He cried and called till it was dark, and then he lay down on the ground, and Caper lay down close beside him. It was not long before Willie cried himself to sleep.

13. When he awoke it was morning, and he began to think of a way to get out. The little writing book that his aunt had given him, was in his pocket. He took it out, and, after a good deal of trouble, wrote the letter to his father.

14. Then he tore the leaf out, and took a string out of his pocket, and tied it round Caper's neck, and tied the letter to the

string. Then he lifted the dog up, and helped him out, and said to him, "Go home, Caper, go home!" The little dog scampered away, and was soon at home.

DEFINITIONS.—1. Bīrth'dāy, *the same day of the month in which a person was born, in each succeeding year.* 5. Neigh'-bor hŏŏd, *the surrounding region which lies nearest, vicinity.* Wom'en (wĭm'en), *plural of woman.* 8. Shȧft, *a deep hole made in the earth, usually for mining purposes.* 14. Seăm'-pered, *ran briskly.*

LESSON LXXII.

THE PERT CHICKEN.

1. There was once a pretty chicken;
　　But his friends were very few,
For he thought that there was nothing
　　In the world but what he knew:
So he always, in the farmyard,
　　Had a very forward way,
Telling all the hens and turkeys
　　What they ought to do and say.
"Mrs. Goose," he said, "I wonder
　　That your goslings you should let
Go out paddling in the water;
　　It will kill them to get wet."

2. "I wish, my old Aunt Dorking,"
　　He began to her, one day,
"That you would n't sit all summer
　　In your nest upon the hay.
Wo n't you come out to the meadow,
　　Where the grass with seeds is filled?"
"If I should," said Mrs. Dorking,
　　"Then my eggs would all get chilled."
"No, they wo n't," replied the chicken,
　　"And no matter if they do;
Eggs are really good for nothing;
　　What's an egg to me or you?"

3. "What's an egg!" said Mrs. Dorking,
　　"Can it be you do not know

You yourself were in an eggshell
    Just one little month ago?
And, if kind wings had not warmed you,
    You would not be out to-day,
Telling hens, and geese, and turkeys,
    What they ought to do and say!

4. "To be very wise, and show it,
        Is a pleasant thing, no doubt;
    But, when young folks talk to old folks,
        They should know what they're about."

Marian Douglas.

DEFINITIONS.—1. Färm′yärd, *the inclosed ground attached to a barn and other farm buildings.* Fôr′ward, *bold, confident.* Tûr′key, *a large domestic fowl.* Gŏṣ′lingṣ, *young geese.* Păd′- dling, *beating the water with the feet, swimming.* 2. Dôr′king, *a species of chicken.*

LESSON LXXIII.

INDIAN CORN.

1. Few plants are more useful to man than Indian corn, or maize. No grain, except rice, is used to so great an extent as an article of food. In some countries corn is almost the only food eaten by the people.

2. Do you know why it is called Indian corn? It is because the American Indians were the first corn growers. Columbus found this grain widely cultivated by them when he discovered the New World. They pounded it in rude, stone bowls, and thus made a coarse flour, which they mixed with water and baked.

3. Indian corn is now the leading crop in the United States. In whatever part of this land we live, we see corn growing every year in its proper season. Yet how few can tell the most simple and important facts about its planting and its growth!

4. Corn, to do well, must have a rich soil and a warm climate. It is a tender plant, and is easily injured by cold weather. The seed corn does not sprout, but rots, if the ground is cold and wet.

5. To prepare land properly for planting corn, the soil is made fine by plowing, and furrows are run across the field four feet apart each way. At every point where these furrows cross, the farmer drops from four to seven grains of seed corn. These are then covered with about two inches of earth, and thus form "hills" of corn.

6. In favorable weather, the tender blades push through the ground in ten days or two weeks; then the stalks mount up rapidly, and the long, streamer-like leaves unfold gracefully from day to day. Corn must be carefully cultivated while the plants are small. After they begin to shade the ground, they need but little hoeing or plowing.

7. The moisture and earthy matter, drawn through the roots, become sap. This passes through the stalk, and enters the leaves. There a great change takes place, which results in the starting of the ears and the growth of the grain.

8. The maize plant bears two kinds of flowers,—male and female. The two are widely separated. The male flowers are on the tassel; the fine silk threads which surround the ear, and peep out from the end of the husks, are the female flowers.

9. Each grain on the cob is the starting-point for a thread of silk; and, unless the thread receives some particle of the dust which falls from the tassel flowers, the kernel with which it is connected will not grow.

10. The many uses of Indian corn and its products are worthy of note. The green

stalks and leaves make excellent fodder for cattle. The ripe grain is used all over the earth as food for horses, pigs, and poultry. Nothing is better for fattening stock.

11. Green corn, or "roasting ears," hulled corn and hominy, New England hasty pudding, and succotash are favorite dishes with many persons. Then there are parched corn and pop corn—the delight of long winter evenings.

12. Cornstarch is an important article of commerce. Sirup and sugar are made from the juice of the stalk, and oil and alcohol from the ripened grain. Corn husks are largely used for filling mat-

tresses, and are braided into mats, baskets, and other useful articles.

13. Thus it will be seen how varied are the uses of Indian corn. And besides being so useful, the plant is very beautiful. The sight of a large cornfield in the latter part of summer, with all its green banners waving and its tasseled plumes nodding, is one to admire, and not to be forgotten.

DEFINITIONS.—1. Ar'ti ele, *a particular one of various things.* 2. Cŭl'ti vāt ed, *grown.* 3. Im pôr'tant, *of much value.* 5. Fŭr'row, *a trench made by a plow.* 6. Fā'vor a ble, *that which is kindly, propitious.* Strēam'er, *a long, narrow flag.* 7. Mois'-ture, *wet, dampness.* Re şŭlts', *comes out, ends.* 8. Sĕp'a rat ed, *apart, not connected.* 9. Pär'ti ele, *a very small portion.* 10. Ex'çel lent, *good, superior.* Fŏd'der, *such food for animals as hay, straw, and vegetables.* Pōul'try, *barnyard fowls.* Sŭe'eo-tăsh, *corn and beans boiled together.* 12. Cŏm'merçe, *trade.* Al'eo hol, *distilled liquor.* Măt'tress eş, *beds stuffed with hair, straw, or other soft material.* Brāid'ed, *woven or twisted together.*

LESSON LXXIV.

THE SNOWBIRD'S SONG.

1. The ground was all covered with snow one day,
   And two little sisters were busy at play,
   When a snowbird was sitting close by on a tree,
   And merrily singing his chick-a-de-dee.

2. He had not been singing that tune very long
    Ere Emily heard him, so loud was his song:
    "O sister, look out of the window!" said she;
    "Here's a dear little bird singing chick-a-de-dee.

3. "Poor fellow! he walks in the snow and the sleet,
    And has neither stockings nor shoes on his feet:
    I wonder what makes him so full of his glee;
    He's all the time singing his chick-a-de-dee.

4. "If I were a barefooted snowbird, I know,
    I would not stay out in the cold and the snow;
    I pity him so! oh, how cold he must be!
    And yet he keeps singing his chick-a-de-dee.

5. "O mother; do get him some stockings, and shoes,
   And a nice little frock, and a hat if he choose:
   I wish he 'd come into the parlor, and see
   How warm we would make him, poor chick-a-de-
      dee!"

6. The bird had flown down for some sweet crumbs of
      bread,
   And heard every word little Emily said:
   "What a figure I 'd make in that dress," thought he,
   And laughed as he warbled his chick-a-de-dee.

7. "I am grateful," said he, "for the wish you express,
   But have no occasion for such a fine dress;
   I rather remain with my little limbs free,
   Than to hobble about, singing chick-a-de-dee.

8. "There is One, my dear child, though I can not
      tell who,
   Has clothed me already, and warm enough, too.
   Good morning! Oh, who are so happy as we?"
   And away he flew, singing his chick-a-de-dee.

                                    F. C. Woodworth.

DEFINITIONS.—1. Chĭck'-a-dē-dee, *an imitation of the notes
of the snowbird.* 6. Fĭg'ūre, *shape, appearance.* 7. Ex prĕss',
make known, declare. Hŏb'ble, *to walk with a hitch or hop.*

MOUNTAINS.

1. The Himalayas are the highest mountains on our globe. They are in Asia, and separate India from Thibet. They extend in a continuous line for more than a thousand miles.

2. If you ever ascend one of these mountains from the plain below, you will have to cross an unhealthy border, twenty miles in width. It is, in fact, a swamp caused by the waters overflowing the river banks.

3. The soil of this swampy border is covered with trees and shrubs, where the tiger, the elephant, and other animals find secure retreat. Beyond this border, you will reach smiling valleys and noble forests.

4. As you advance onward and upward, you will get among bolder and more rugged scenes. The sides of the mountains are very steep, sometimes well wooded to quite a height, but sometimes quite barren.

5. In crossing a river you must be content with three ropes for a bridge. You will find the streets of the towns to be simply stairs

cut out of the rock, and see the houses rising
in tiers.

6. The pathways into Thibet, among these
mountains, are mere tracks by the side of

foaming torrents. Often, as you advance, you
will find every trace of the path swept away
by the falling of rocks and earth from above.

7. Sometimes you will find posts driven into the mountain side, upon which branches of trees and earth are spread. This forms a trembling foothold for the traveler.

8. In the Andes, in South America, the sure-footed mule is used to carry travelers. Quite often a chasm must be crossed that is many feet wide and hundreds of feet deep. The mule will leap across this chasm, but not until it is sure it can make a safe jump.

9. "One day," says a traveler, "I went by the worst pass over the Andes Mountains. The path for seventy yards was very narrow, and at one point it was washed entirely away. On one side the rock brushed my shoulder, and on the other side my foot overhung the precipice."

10. The guide told this man, after he was safely over the pass, that, to his knowledge, four hundred mules had fallen over that precipice, and in many instances travelers had lost their lives at that terrible spot.

DEFINITIONS. — 1. Hĭm ä'la ya, *also written* Him mä'lĕh. Thĭb'et (Tĭb-), *a country of central Asia.* 2. As çĕnd', *go up, climb.* Swạmp, *low, wet ground.* 3. Re trēat', *place of safety.* 4. Ad vȧnçe', *go forward.* Rŭg'ḡed, *rough.* Băr'ren, *without trees or shrubs, unproductive.* 5. Tiёrṣ, *rows one above another.*

7. Fŏŏt'hōld, *that on which one may tread.* 8. An'dēṣ, *next to the highest range of mountains in the world.* Ċhăṣm (kăzm), *a deep opening in the earth, or cleft in the rocks.* 9. Prĕç'i pĭçe, *a very steep and dangerous descent.* 10. Knŏwl'-edġe (nŏl'ej), *that which is known.*

LESSON LXXVI.

A CHILD'S HYMN.

1. God make my life a little light,
    Within the world to glow;
  A little flame that burneth bright
    Wherever I may go.

2. God make my life a little flower,
    That giveth joy to all,
  Content to bloom in native bower,
    Although its place be small.

3. God make my life a little song,
    That comforteth the sad;
  That helpeth others to be strong,
    And makes the singer glad.

4. God make my life a little hymn
    Of tenderness and praise;
  Of faith—that never waxeth dim
    In all His wondrous ways.

LESSON LXXVII.

HOLDING THE FORT.

1. While Genie was walking slowly down street one day, she heard an odd rapping on the pavement behind her. Looking round, she saw Rob Grey hobbling on crutches.

2. "Why, what is the matter?" cried Genie. "I haven't seen you for a week, and now you are walking in that way."

3. "I shall have to walk in this way as much as a week longer, Genie. I sprained my ankle by stopping too quick—no, not too quick, either, for there was something in my way."

"What was it?" asked Genie.

4. "One of the Commandments," replied Rob. "You remember how that lecturer talked to us about 'holding the fort'? Well, I thought I should like to do it; but it's a pretty long war, you know—all a lifetime, and no vacations—furloughs, I think they call them."

5. "If there was nothing to fight, we should not need to be soldiers," said Genie.

6. "Well, I thought I would try; but the

first day, when we came out of the schoolhouse, Jack Lee snatched my books out of
my hand, and threw them into the mud.

7. "I started after him as fast as I could
run. I meant to throw him where he had

thrown the books, when, all of a sudden, I
thought of the Commandment about return-
ing good for evil.

8. "I stopped short—so short, that, some-

how, my foot twisted under me. So, you see, it was one of the Commandments."

9. "If one must stumble at them, it is a good thing to fall on the right side," said Genie, with a wise nod of her head.

10. "The whole thing puzzles me, and makes me feel—well, like giving it up," said Rob. "It might have served me right when I was chasing Jack; but when I thought of the Commandment, I really tried to do the right thing."

11. "You did do it, Rob," said Genie. "You 'held the fort' that time. Why, don't you see—you are only a wounded soldier."

12. "I never thought of that," said Rob. "If I believe that way— " He began to whistle, and limped off to school without finishing the sentence. But Genie knew, by the way he behaved that day, that he had made up his mind to *hold the fort*.

DEFINITIONS.—1. Pāve′ment, *a walk covered with brick or other hard material.* Crŭtch′eş, *long sticks with crosspieces at the top, to aid lame persons in walking.* 3. Sprāined, *injured by wrenching or twisting.* 4. Com mȧnd′ments, *holy laws recorded in the Bible.* Lĕc′tur er, *a public speaker.* Va eā′tion, *the time between two school terms.* Fûr′lough (fûr′lo), *a soldier's leave of absence.* 11. Wound′ed (wōōnd′ed), *hurt, injured.* 12. Be hāved′, *acted.*

LESSON LXXVIII.

THE LITTLE PEOPLE.

1. A dreary place would be this earth,
   Were there no little people in it;
   The song of life would lose its mirth,
   Were there no children to begin it;

2. No little forms, like buds to grow,
   And make the admiring heart surrender;
   No little hands on breast and brow,
   To keep the thrilling love chords tender.

3. The sterner souls would grow more stern,
   Unfeeling nature more inhuman,
   And man to utter coldness turn,
   And woman would be less than woman.

4. Life's song, indeed, would lose its charm,
   Were there no babies to begin it;
   A doleful place this world would be,
   Were there no little people in it.

John G. Whittier.

DEFINITIONS.—1. Drēar'y, *cheerless.* 2. Sur rĕn'der, *give up, yield.* Lȯve ehȯrdṣ, *ties of affection.* 3. Stērn, *severe, harsh.* Ut'ter, *complete.* 4. Dōle'fṳl, *gloomy, sad.*

LESSON LXXIX.

GOOD NIGHT.

1. The sun is hidden from our sight,
    The birds are sleeping sound;
  'T is time to say to all, "Good night!"
    And give a kiss all round.

2. Good night, my father, mother, dear!
    Now kiss your little son;
  Good night, my friends, both far and near!
    Good night to every one.

3. Good night, ye merry, merry birds!
    Sleep well till morning light;
  Perhaps, if you could sing in words,
    You would have said, "Good night!"

4. To all my pretty flowers, good night!
    You blossom while I sleep;
  And all the stars, that shine so bright,
    With you their watches keep.

5. The moon is lighting up the skies,
    The stars are sparkling there;
  'T is time to shut our weary eyes,
    And say our evening prayer.

Mrs. Follen.